MATZOH BALLS AND BASEBALLS

CONVERSATIONS WITH JEWISH FORMER MAJOR LEAGUE BASEBALL PLAYERS

Dave Cohen

Havenhurst Books

Copyright © 2010 Dave Cohen

ISBN 978-0-9822853-4-3, 0-9822853-4-5

Printed in the United States of America

Baseball card images courtesy of the Topps Company, Inc.

Card images of Jim Gaudet and Morris Savransky courtesy of
    Jewish Major Leaguers, Inc.

Foreword image courtesy of Steve Greenberg

Cover design – Andrew Harmon

For my ball club: Carol, Sam, and Jack

CONTENTS

Seventeen Jewish Ball Players: Fighting Bigotry, Establishing Pride

Baseball is the only sport that has, as one of its statistics, things that people have done wrong. That column in the box score is called "errors." There is something uniquely Jewish about keeping score of where you have gone wrong. There's no shame in it. You just keep score of your errors, either for the record books (in Major League Baseball) or for Yom Kippur (in Judaism). What is it about baseball that has fascinated Jews for the past century? Maybe it's because baseball was deemed the ultimate "America's Pastime." In so many ways, Major League Baseball *is* America, and the immigrant Jews arriving in the early 20th century wanted nothing more than to be American.

Every Jew, of course, knows about the great Jewish baseball stars: Hank Greenberg in the 1940's, Sandy Koufax in the 1960's, and even Shawn Green in recent years. But what many Americans (and Jewish Americans) do not know is that between 150 and 200 Jews have played professional baseball during the past 100 years. Each generation of immigrants and ethnic groups have made baseball their own. To read the names of the baseball stars over the past 80 years is to see the emerging landscape of ethnicity in America, from Babe Ruth (German), to Greenberg (Jewish), to DiMaggio (Italian), to Hank Aaron (African-American), to Alex Rodriquez (Dominican) to today's South American and Japanese stars. Every group has wanted to claim baseball as its own. And so it is, every cultural, ethnic and racial group has its baseball stories to tell.

Dave Cohen has taken up the task of telling the stories of seventeen Jews who played the game. They are the stories of seventeen Jewish boys who swung a bat, held a glove, caught a fly, or fielded a grounder. If you are a baseball lover, then you will read this book to learn more about some of its more obscure players. And if you are Jewish, you will read this book with pride, for what seventeen young Jews had done over the years representing themselves and their faith, establishing pride and combating bigotry against the Jews.

Rabbi Steven Lebow
Senior Rabbi
Temple Kol Emeth
Marietta, Georgia

Remembering My Father

Steve Greenberg

"When I was playing, I used to resent being singled out as a Jewish baseball player. I wanted to be known as a great ballplayer, period. . . . Lately though, I find myself wanting to be remembered not only as a great baseball player, but even more as a great Jewish ballplayer."—Hall of Famer Hank Greenberg

My dad was a huge influence on me, as I suspect most fathers are on their sons. What he did not do was to push me in the direction of baseball. My love of baseball came, more or less, as a matter of osmosis. I was obviously around it a lot. I knew that my dad had been a player. He had retired before I was born. He was the General Manager of the Cleveland Indians when I was growing up, so baseball was central to our lives, but it wasn't an overt push on his part that moved me in that direction. I really learned to appreciate baseball and follow baseball and play baseball on my own initiative.

Later in my life, in my dad's later years, for the first time I really reflected on what he meant as a baseball player, as a Jewish icon, for a whole generation in the 1930's and 1940's and, for that matter, the historical context in which he played and rose to fame. There's just such a huge contrast between the times that existed when my dad played as opposed to when I played, which was the 1970's. Today, with Ryan Braun and Kevin Youkilis and the Jewish players out there, it's not out of the ordinary that a Jew could be a professional athlete, a professional baseball player, even potentially a Hall of Famer or an All-Star. In my dad's day, that was such an oddity and rare occurrence, which puts into perspective his legacy and is so much a part of what set him apart from so many other people in that era. Frankly, it is amazing to me that he was able to accomplish what he did at the height of worldwide anti-Semitism (and that includes here at home) in the 1930's. By the time I played, there would be the occasional taunt, but nothing like what my dad went through. While there weren't all that many Jewish players in my day, there were a handful, certainly playing in college ball as I did. And then you look at today and being a Jewish ballplayer, it is almost like being an Italian-American ballplayer or a Polish-American ballplayer, there's a whole bunch of them. It is sort of accepted that Jews can play baseball. I attribute some of that to Sandy Koufax, going back more to my era, who was such a big part of reinforcing the notion that the Jews could play ball and be All-Stars and Hall of Fame-quality players breaking those old stereotypes. I would say today that those stereotypes aren't totally gone, but for the most part, they are, and my dad's legacy is an important part of that change.

Not long ago, I spoke to a group of seventh graders, kids around twelve or thirteen years old, at my synagogue. This is a group that elected to study, as part of their after school program, the impact of Jews on sports, particularly baseball in America. When I went in to speak to them, the first question I asked was, if you went home and told your parents that you thought you wanted to be a professional baseball player, how many of you think that your parents would be pleased with that? And every one of them raised their hand. I was there to talk about my dad and my experiences, so I told the kids a family story. I said, well, imagine my father, in his time. The first line in his autobiography is: "People in my neighborhood used to say, 'Mrs. Greenberg has such nice kids. It's too bad one of them had to grow up and be a bum. I was the bum.'" Think about that: seventy years ago, for a Jew to be an athlete or a baseball player, he was considered the next thing to a bum, and now every kid in the class thinks that their parents would be thrilled that they were going to go out and be ballplayers. That's really how times have changed. My sports career came in the middle of that change in the 1960's and 1970's and as an agent in the 1980's and a baseball executive in the 1990's. I've watched that happen, and I feel very good about it.

In my dad's later years, he and I talked a lot about how he approached his career early on and how he looked back on his impact on the game and on Jews in sports.

From those conversations, I came to appreciate what he had meant and how he felt about his early career. When he came up, he just wanted to get established in the big leagues. Like every other kid who signs a professional contract, his first goal was just to get to the big leagues. Then, once he got there, his next goal was to make the starting line-up on the team and, of course, to keep improving. My dad was a very, very competitive guy as an athlete. He was driven, not to perfection, but to improve himself and to be as good as he could be. Looking back—this was all way before I was even born—I can well understand how his total focus was on improving himself.

He told me a story once about when he came up as a rookie. He sat on the bench and was very disgruntled that he was not playing. Finally, he went back to the minors and then came back again and got to play in the big league. In 1933 he was the starting first baseman for the Tigers and he hit a little over .300. He hadn't quite hit his stride as a power hitter, but he had a decent year. The next year, he had a terrific year. The team won the pennant, lost to the Cardinals in the World Series, but he went home that year feeling really good, having established himself as a key part of this pennant-winning team. He told me that he went to spring training the next year, 1935, really as a twenty-four-year-old kid, and he remembered one day, early in spring training when they were playing the Dodgers in an exhibition game, he looked around the field, at the Dodger team, and he realized that there wasn't a single player on the Brooklyn team that was better than he was. This was him talking to himself. He said that's when he realized that he was no longer just struggling to make the team or to become a starter. He was now at a different level. And that's how he felt in terms of his confidence at that point in time. That's when the comparisons between him and Lou Gehrig began, and then, of course, three years later he challenged Babe Ruth's record. Here he was being compared to Lou Gehrig and Babe Ruth. Joe DiMaggio had come into the league; Ted Williams had come into the league, and Hank Greenberg's name was bandied about with the top players in the league.

In my office I have a photograph, actually a fairly famous photograph, taken at the 1937 All-Star game. There are seven American Leaguers standing and holding their bats at the stadium. Starting from the left it's Lou Gehrig, Joe Cronin, Bill Dickey, Joe DiMaggio, Charlie Gehringer, Jimmie Foxx, and my dad. So that was the American League lineup, or at least seven members of it for that All-Star game. When you think about that, all Hall of Famers ultimately, my dad wasn't thinking about, "Am I the best Jewish player?" He was thinking about, "Am I the best player? Am I the best first baseman? How do I compare to Gehrig and Foxx?" So that really was his mentality and mindset throughout his playing career. If you fast forward to when he was in his sixties and seventies, well past his playing days, those competitive juices having sort of abated a little bit, and he had a chance to reflect back on his career, I think what struck him was the number of people who came up to him, or who wrote him letters asking for his autograph, and part of their message was: "I remember my father telling me what an inspiration you were to our people and how proud our community was of you and your accomplishments and how you conducted yourself as a gentleman and shed a positive light on all of the Jews in the community." I think that message began to sink in, and in his more reflective moments, he came to understand that beyond the comparisons with Ruth and Gehrig and Foxx, what he meant as a symbol or as a beacon to the Jewish people really was important. He was a modest guy who very seldom talked about that publicly, but I think that's what he came to realize over the years.

So what did my dad mean to baseball and to Jewish baseball players? I think it's important for any community, whether it's the Italian-American community, the Armenian-American community, or the Jewish-American community, to maintain that sense of community and pride. We're all Americans first. I'm speaking for myself and for my dad. First and foremost we're Americans, but then we do have some sort of other sense of connection. In the case of Jewish-Americans especially, who came here as immigrants, for the most part from difficult circumstances in Europe or the Middle East or Northern Africa or wherever it may have been, for that whole generation that came from Europe, chased out by one regime or another, with just the shirts on their back and built a community here in the U.S., having that sense of community is a big part of what makes this country special. The same is true for the Irish, for the Italians and for other immigrants.

Celebrating that within your community, whether it's to celebrate the great athletes from your heritage, the great scientists, the great artists, I think that's important for any community, not just Jews. It is part of the American heritage, having that sense of pride in your people and how they contribute to the great American society.

Steve Greenberg was the captain of the Yale baseball team. He spent five years in the minor leagues in the Washington Senators/Texas Rangers organization. A lawyer who represented dozens of Major League players, he became deputy commissioner of Major League Baseball from 1990 until 1993. He left the league to found the Classic Sports Network. For more on Hank Greenberg and his legacy, see Aviva Kempner's award-winning documentary The Life and Times of Hank Greenberg *(1998) or Hank Greenberg's autobiography,* Hank Greenberg: The Story of My Life *(with Ira Berkow, 2001).*

INTRODUCTION

If you are Jewish and a baseball fan, or even a fan of sports in general, there is no doubt you have heard the well known joke numerous times. You know, the one about the book of great Jewish athletes: "It's a pamphlet." That got me to thinking. When it comes to Major League Baseball, are Hank Greenberg and Sandy Koufax the only two Jewish players to have ever left their mark on the national pastime? Who did all the Jewish baseball fans root for?

During the period of what was then called the New Immigration from Europe, between 1875 and 1920, more than twenty million people passed through Ellis Island in New York and settled into cities across the country. Not surprisingly, many of these new Americans were attracted to the game of baseball. Divided into different sections of the various cities in which they settled, ethnocentrism and ethnic pride flourished among these people who now found themselves living among others of different cultural backgrounds. When it came to baseball, for example, the Italian communities had well known players to follow and cheer for like Joe DiMaggio, Dom DiMaggio, Yogi Berra, Tony Lazzeri, Sal "The Barber" Maglie as well as numerous others. Early on in the Negro leagues and then beginning in 1947, African American fans had Jackie Robinson, Larry Doby, Monte Irvin, Henry Aaron, Willie Mays, Ernie Banks, Satchel Paige, Roy Campanella, Elston Howard and latter day Hall of Fame caliber players like Eddie Murray, Willie Stargell, Tony Gwynn, Dave Winfield and Jim Rice. Latino fans had the likes of Roberto Clemente, Luis Aparicio, Orlando Cepeda, the Alou brothers, Orestes "Minnie" Minoso as well as guys like Dave Concepcion and Tony Perez. In recent years you are more likely to see fans waving flags in support of their favorite players from places like the Dominican Republic, Puerto Rico, and Venezuela and more recently the growing number of players from Japan and Korea.

So, who did the Jewish fans follow with pride in the same manner that African Americans followed Jackie Robinson? History tells us that Jewish baseball players reached the professional ranks as early as the late 1800's with two of the better known players being Erskine Mayer and Barney Pelty, though it is believed that a player by the name of Lipman Pike was the first Jewish player in the 1870's. Mayer had an eight-year career between 1912 and 1919, playing for the Philadelphia Phillies, Pittsburgh Pirates, and Chicago White Sox. Considered one of the best

Jewish pitchers ever, he had a career record of 91-70 with a 2.96 ERA and 482 strikeouts. His older brother, Sam Mayer, also made the majors, appearing in eleven games for the Washington Nationals in 1915. It was Erskine Mayer who surrendered Honus Wagner's 3,000th hit in 1914. He was a twenty game winner in 1914 and 1915. He finished his career in 1920, playing in one game for the Minor League Atlanta Crackers. Pelty, nicknamed "The Yiddish Curver," was one of the first Jewish baseball players in the American League. Like Mayer, Pelty was also a pitcher. He played for the St. Louis Browns and the Washington Senators between 1903 and 1912. He enjoyed his best season in 1906, when he went 16-11 with an ERA of 1.59. His career ERA was 2.63, ranking him first among all Jewish pitchers with Koufax second. He still ranks 60th overall in Major League Baseball pitcher rankings.

A few other notable names of that era include Morris "Moe" Berg, Harry Danning, Sid Gordon, and Al Rosen. Berg became better known for his activity off the field. Following a fifteen-year career in the major leagues, 1923 to 1939, Berg traveled the world working as a spy for the Office of Strategic Services during World War II. Berg, a graduate of both Princeton University and Columbia Law School, was the subject of the 1994 Nicholas Dawidoff biography, *The Catcher Was a Spy: The Mysterious Life of Moe Berg*. Danning spent his entire career with the New York Giants (1933 to 1942). He was a member of four straight National League All-Star teams (1938-1941) and a member of the 1933 Giants team that beat the Washington Senators in the World Series. Gordon played thirteen seasons, between 1941 and 1955, with the New York Giants, Boston/Milwaukee Braves, and the Pittsburgh Pirates. He ranks third all-time among Jewish baseball players in home runs, behind Hank Greenberg and Shawn Green. In his first full season with the Cleveland Indians in 1950, Rosen hit 37 home runs, which was more than any American League rookie had hit up until that time. Then in 1953 he missed baseball's Triple Crown by one percentage point, hitting .336 (Mickey Vernon won the batting title at .337) while amassing 43 home runs and 145 RBI's. On and off the field, Rosen, at one time an amateur boxer, was not one to stand by idle while being the object of anti-Semitic verbal attacks and was known to challenge those spewing the insults. Many Jewish fans looked up to Rosen just for this reason as he defied the common stereotype of the Jew as being weak and cowardly.

We've read and heard the stories about Greenberg and Koufax. They are the only two Jewish players in the Hall of Fame and are the only ones to have "household name" status. Koufax, the young hurler with a blazing and sometimes out of control fastball, joined the Dodgers when they still called Ebbets Field in Brooklyn their home. It was in Los Angeles where he became one of the most dominant pitchers of his era. There he was finally able to gain some control of his pitches with the help of another Jewish teammate, catcher Norm Sherry, whose story you'll hear in this book, including the tale of Koufax's steadfast refusal to play on the Jewish High Holiday, Yom Kippur, which further increased his prominence in Jewish communities throughout the country. Unfortunately, arm problems shortened his career. Koufax, who mostly stays out of the public eye, has watched his legendary status increase as each season passes.

Decades earlier, in the 30's and 40's, Hank Greenberg was a similar beacon for the Jewish baseball fans. He was tagged with the nickname "Hammerin' Hank" long before Henry Aaron adopted it. Greenberg, like Koufax, was also one of the first Jewish athletes to bring attention to their religion, even though he was not very observant. In 1934 he refused to play on Yom Kippur, despite the fact that the Tigers were still in the American League pennant race. As it was, he became legendary as a member of the Detroit Tigers after almost signing with the Yankees. New York tried to sign him in 1929, but Greenberg, a first baseman, was well aware that they already had a capable player at that position who did not take days off. That particular player was Lou Gehrig. Can you imagine Greenberg wearing pinstripes alongside the great Yankee players of that time? Baseball historians refer to the 1927 Yankees and their offensive prowess. Adding Greenberg's bat to the lineup of those great Yankee teams of that era would have certainly been exciting to watch. He would have been huge with the large New York Jewish community. From interviews following his playing days, Greenberg came to realize how special it was to have been a great Jewish ballplayer.

There are other notables who have played professional baseball over the years, including the game's first Designated Hitter and the "other" Jewish Cy Young Award winner. Ron Blomberg's bat is on display at the Baseball Hall of Fame in Cooperstown after he walked to the plate at Boston's Fenway Park on April 6, 1973 and became the game's first-ever DH, facing the Red Sox' Luis Tiant and drawing a walk. Blomberg's name is so tied to the event that he aptly titled his 2006 autobiography, *Designated Hebrew: The Ron Blomberg Story*. Blomberg, like others before him who played in New York, enjoyed the celebrity status that came with being a Jewish ballplayer in The Big Apple. Steve Stone, who was a teammate of Blomberg's on the White Sox in 1978, is the answer to another good Jewish baseball trivia question. Who are the only two Jewish pitchers to have won the Cy Young Award? Obviously Koufax was the first and, if you were not aware, Stone was the other. Pitching for the Baltimore Orioles in 1980, Stone went 25-7 and, along with the Cy Young award, also won *The Sporting News* Pitcher of the Year award. Stone became even better known in his post-baseball career broadcasting work alongside Harry Caray on the Chicago Cubs television broadcasts on WGN.

During the 1970's Ken Holtzman was one of the most dominating pitchers to take the mound. As part of a staff that featured Jim "Catfish" Hunter and Vida Blue, Holtzman won a total of 77 games with Oakland between 1972 and 1975. Along with other greats like Reggie Jackson, Bert Campaneris, and Rollie Fingers, he was a part of three A's World Series champion teams. A memorable game for Holtzman occurred in 1966 when, after initially being compared to Sandy Koufax early in his career, he actually got to face him. On September 26th, while with the Cubs, he pitched opposite Koufax one day after both sat out for Yom Kippur.

Holtzman was a teammate of another Jewish slugger, Mike Epstein, while in Oakland. A memorable event took place in 1972 during the baseball playoffs, when Holtzman, Epstein and Reggie Jackson each wore a black armband in memory of the eleven Israeli athletes who were murdered by terrorists at the Olympic Games in Munich. As for Mike Epstein, who was given the nickname "Super Jew" by an opposing manager while still in the minor leagues, he also enjoyed an eventful career. As a college All-American at Cal-Berkeley, he was a member of the first U.S. Olympic baseball team in 1964 that won the gold medal. Later on, one of the highlights of his career was when he played with the Washington Senators (1967-1971). Even thought they were a ball club that struggled to win games, they were managed by Hall of Fame legend Ted Williams, who became a mentor for Epstein. It was then that Epstein developed his keen interest in the science of hitting. Today, Epstein is a professional hitting instructor based in Colorado.

It was at a book signing hosted by author Rob Trucks that first gave me the idea for this project. His book, *Cup of Coffee: The Very Short Careers of Eighteen Major League Pitchers*, featured the stories of former players who had spent just a short time in the majors. At his signing, one of the players interviewed for his book, Larry Yellen, was there. Even as long time baseball fan, I was not familiar with Yellen's career. From talking with him I learned that he was Jewish. While thinking about the chance encounter a little while later, I wondered just how many other Jewish players there were whose careers I was not familiar with. So that's when I took an interest in researching and learning about them.

I must say that of all the former players that I interviewed for this book, in my opinion, Steve Stone was the one who "got it." By that I mean that he understood why I was working on this project and why it's important to recognize the accomplishments of Jewish ball players. I've said many times that Judaism is not a "race," it's a religion. However, for whatever reason, by many non-Jews, Jews are treated and viewed like a racial minority. With that being said, because of the history and the struggles of the Jewish people across the globe over the years, there is a sense of camaraderie among many Jews, whether they know one another or not. In some instances it doesn't even matter how religiously observant one is. There is for many, although certainly not all, a certain bond that you share if you're Jewish. So, for all the fans out there who might only know of Sandy Koufax or Hank Greenberg, this book is here to briefly introduce you to some of the other Jewish players who left their marks on the national past time. It's estimated that between 160 and 175 Jews have played Major League Baseball. What follows is a few of their compelling stories.

"When I was on the mound pitching against the batter, I was in control, but obviously, Roberto Clemente wasn't just any hitter and it shook me up a little bit."

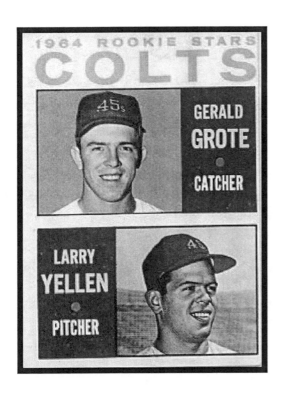

LARRY YELLEN

Larry Yellen *grew up in Brooklyn, playing ball on the streets, all the while growing to love the game of baseball. He graduated from Lafayette High School, the same school that had graduated Sandy Koufax four years earlier. Growing up in a Jewish household in the 1950's, Larry's parents had ideas other than baseball as a career for their son. After some unproductive time spent at Hunter College in New York, Yellen's parents acquiesced, and he soon embarked on his career in professional baseball. Yellen was twenty when he broke into the big leagues on September 26, 1963, after signing as an undrafted amateur free agent with the Houston Colt .45s in 1962. Larry spent part of two seasons in Houston, Texas with the Colt .45s, who later became the Astros. He pitched in a total of fourteen Major League games, made two starts, totaled twenty-six innings pitched with twelve strikeouts and eleven walks and an ERA of 6.23. He had five at-bats with no hits and one strikeout. Yellen played his final game on October 3, 1964. He lives in Duluth, Georgia.*

Tell me about your early years growing up in Brooklyn, and how you came to love the game of baseball.

LY: Well, it was really sports in general. I knew what to do with a baseball when I was three years old. My uncle, Aaron Dultz, was basically the one who taught me how to throw and catch a baseball when I was three and four years old. I was excited about it because I did it as good as kids who were five, six, seven years old. He used to put us around in a semi-circle, a bunch of my friends along with myself, he would toss the ball to each of us and we'd throw it back to him. I got excited because I caught the ball more often than the other kids did. I threw the ball harder than the other kids did and they were all older than I was. Now, if you ask me what part did my dad play? My dad I hardly got to see me because he worked from three o'clock in the afternoon to three o'clock in the morning and had to travel from Brooklyn all the way in to Newark, New Jersey. So, he was unable to help me but, again, my uncle was the one that really got me started in the game. As I got older, I was playing with kids that were five years older than I was because that's the kind of talent I was born with. One thing led to another, and I got into high school and I was a member of the Lafayette High School baseball team when I was a freshman, which was unheard of back in those days. I did fairly well, as you can imagine, and went on to become a professional.

During the time you were playing in high school, did you have any thoughts about whether or not you could go on and play baseball at a higher level, be it college or the major leagues?

LY: In high school, I had absolutely no desire to do anything but go right to the major leagues, and I honestly believed that it was just going to be a question of time. I did real well in high school. I was MVP in high school in New York and I had no reason not to believe that I'd be good enough, but there were a couple of stumbling blocks in the way, if you will. My Jewish parents, for one thing. I'm the middle of three brothers, my oldest brother is a psychiatrist, my younger brother is a Ph.D. in mathematics (he has written two books), and I'm the schnook in the middle. Even though I was good at what I was doing on the ball field, there was no question in my parents' minds that I wasn't doing *that* before I went to college and got a degree. And so, here I am. I graduated high school. I've got some scouts that are looking at me to sign me up and get me started on a professional career, and I've got my parents in the background saying, "Larry, you're going to college." So I went to college for two years. I went to Hunter College, which was part of the City University of New York, and I was going to prove to my parents that this was the wrong move. I didn't crack a book. I ran a 1.8 GPA. I had to go to the school psychologist in my sophomore year in order to convince the psychologist that it was more detrimental for me not to play baseball because of my low GPA, than it would be to play baseball. I got lucky and he went along with it. But, finally after my sophomore year, and again I repeat the 1.8 GPA, my parents said, "Gee, maybe it's time for him do what he wants to do."

Baseball fans may remember that the great Jewish player Sandy Koufax also came out of Lafayette four years before you. How familiar were you with his accomplishments?

LY: To be honest with you, when I looked at Sandy Koufax, yes, I knew he was Jewish, but I never really thought about it when I looked at him as a Major League Baseball player or even as a high school pitcher. I never looked at it that way. And so, he didn't blaze any paths for me. That I was a pitcher and Jewish, those are the only two things we had in common. We both went to Lafayette and we were both Jewish, there's where it ended. He was by far the greatest pitcher I have ever seen in my whole life; that's how good he was. I didn't look up to him and say to myself, "Boy, I want to be just like him." Anybody would have wanted to be like Sandy Koufax, if he were a pitcher. It didn't matter if you were Jewish or Christian or anything else. It didn't really matter.

If not Sandy Koufax, then how aware were you, if at all, when you were in high school, or even younger, of athletes who were Jewish and playing sports professionally?

LY: I was, but to a very, very small extent. It didn't mean anything to me that some Jewish players were making it all the way up to the top, whether they were playing basketball or baseball or football or whatever. I knew it, but it just didn't play a part in my thought process.

As you mentioned, before you made your way into professional baseball, you went to college for two years. After college, what path did you follow to get into pro baseball?

LY: I guess it's just a mental process and there wasn't much of it that I remember to be honest with you. It was a question of winding up and throwing the ball south as hard as you could or throwing a curve ball that broke as late and as hard as it could or a change-up with good motion. I mean, it didn't matter. If I had those pitches in high school and in college for a couple of years, I was just going to take it with an open mind to a professional career and learn as much as I could and develop into, hopefully, a Major League Baseball player who deserved to be up there and was going to stay for a couple of years.

How was it that you became a pitcher as opposed to a position player?

LY: The strength of my arm. I could throw as far as anybody when I was growing up, at least that's what I was told, and I did it with accuracy. I enjoyed, I guess, being in control of the game, which pitchers are, when they are that good. It was something that I was really attracted to.

Once you signed with the Colt .45s, which Minor League team in their system did they assign you to first?

LY: Right after my sophomore year in 1962, I signed with the Houston organization. 1963 was my first year and spring training was in Apache Junction, Arizona. When we broke camp, I was assigned to the Minor League team in San Antonio, in the Texas League.

So what is it like for you when you leave New York and head out to Arizona for the first time to report to your first Minor League assignment? I'm guessing a little bit of culture shock?

LY: Culture shock. Being on my own. You know, things were different back in those days. When you were eighteen years old and you are the most valuable player in New York State and your parents tell you that you can't play baseball yet because you got to go to college. I mean, if that happened today people would be laughing at the control parents had over kids back in those days. And again, the reason that I'm even mentioning that to you is because that's what kind of a family we had. We were very closely knit in the home. My two brothers that I had, we were all very close, well educated, and to me, to leave the house was a trip in itself. A mental trip because I had never been on my own and here I was going out to be on my own. I wouldn't say it was frightening, and, of course, I don't remember my exact reaction to it, but I was excited about it because I was getting to do something that was the love of my life and that was playing baseball.

Throughout your time in the minor leagues did you ever encounter any confrontational situations, be it name-calling or discriminatory actions, which made you angry or uncomfortable?

LY: There were a couple of incidents. One that happened real early occurred on our first road trip when I was with San Antonio. We're not flying, we're taking really long bus rides, eight, ten, twelve, fourteen hours at a time and here we are, I forget what town we were pulling into, it might have been Albuquerque for all I know, the bus stops at a hotel and all the black people get off and the white people stay on. They go to another hotel, and I was awestruck by the whole thing. I mean, it's probably one of the three top things that I remember going all the way back to my baseball career. I was thinking, "Why is this happening?" Maybe it just shows the level of my naiveté that I had but it struck me, and not in the greatest way.

Everybody knows that there were incidents of racism and anti-Semitism in baseball in those days. Were there any incidents that directly affected you? Did other players know of your Jewish heritage, and if so, did that ever lead to any incidents in either the minor or major leagues?

LY: Yes, there were a couple of things. One occurred at the end of the 1964 season after being up with the Astros for most of the year. They sent me down to get some work because I was just sitting around, pitching in ballgames that we were either up by ten or down by ten runs. Well, we were eating lunch one afternoon, it was towards the end of the season, and we were sitting around, maybe eight or ten of us at the table, and I was talking to a very good friend of mine by the name of Wally Wolf, who lived out West while I was in the East, and I said to Wally, "Anytime you want to call me here's what you do Wally. Call me person-to-person and reverse the charges and when I hear your voice on the phone I will not accept the charges and this way you can call me straight back and you won't have to pay any extra fees for person-to-person and reversing the charges." And lo and behold a right-handed pitcher named Jessie Hickman said to me, "You fucking Jews are all alike. You're always trying to screw somebody out of a dime." I fell into this guy's little trap. Being brought up in a baseball locker room my whole life, I got sucked into it. I started screaming at him about his Southern heritage and blah, blah, blah that he was a moron with a single digit IQ and so on and so forth. The next thing I know I'm being punched in the mouth and knocked off my chair by Hickman. I rushed to get up off the ground, and I threw a punch and hit him in the face and then we were broken up. When we got to the ball park that night my lips were probably six inches away from my face, that's how swollen my lips were. The manager, when I walked into the locker room, said, "How did that happen to you Larry?" Oh, I left out one other detail. I was supposed to pitch that night! He said, "What happened to you Larry?" I said, "I just walked into a wall," because in those days you didn't share this with the upper crust like that and I just kept it to myself and, to be honest with you, I don't remember how many innings I lasted and whether I won the game or lost the game, but obviously that was one of the lowlights of my career in baseball.

You're in San Antonio in 1963 and you played pretty well there. Your record was 8-5 in 18 games with 74 strikeouts and an ERA that was just under three (2.82) and you get called up to join the Colt .45s late that September. Do you remember the first time you walked into that club house and what it was like to play in your first Major League game?

LY: To be honest with you Dave, I don't want to make up any stories. When I found out about getting called up, I know I was so excited. I could not wait to call my parents; I could not wait to call my uncle, that's how excited I was about it. I'm sure that everyone that went up to the major leagues for the first time had similar feelings about it. I mean, it's almost impossible to describe the feeling of getting to the top of your game, or the top of whatever you were pursuing, in such a short period of time.

You made your Major League debut on September 26, 1963 against the Pittsburgh Pirates. As you remember it, tell me what it was like for you to actually walk out on that field for the first time.

LY: Frightening. One of the greatest players that I still remember is Roberto Clemente and I pitched against Roberto Clemente. I don't remember Willie Stargell that well, but I do remember Roberto Clemente. He did get a base hit off of me, as far as I can remember but it was frightening. I mean, when I was on the mound pitching against the batter, I was in control but, obviously, Roberto Clemente wasn't just any hitter and it shook me up a little bit.

You played with some pretty good players as well on the Colt .45s in 1963 and Astros in 1964.

LY: Yes I did. Jimmy Wynn was our center fielder. Joe Morgan was our second baseman. Rusty Staub was our first baseman. Jerry Grote was out catcher. Bob Aspromonte was our third baseman. We had a pretty good team. I didn't know how good all those guys were until years later but they were good.

You mentioned having faced Roberto Clemente. Were there any other memorable pitcher vs. batter experiences for you?

LY: Yes, two guys. One was during the season, I pitched against the Giants. I walked Willie Mays with the bases loaded. In spring training, I forget which one it was, it was either 1964 or 1965 when we were in Cocoa Beach, Florida, I faced Mickey Mantle in the bottom of the ninth in an exhibition game. I was called in to face him with one out, we were up by one run, I threw him one pitch and he hit a rocket, a rocket at Joe Morgan, who flipped to Sonny Jackson back to Rusty Staub at first. Game over. The next day in the newspaper there's this article about this kid from Brooklyn who got Mickey to hit into a game-ending double play. Those two guys, I would say, are Hall of Famers.

It has been well documented in other books written about Hank Greenberg and Sandy Koufax regarding their unwillingness to play during the high Jewish holidays like Yom Kippur. You also found yourself in a similar situation in which you had to make the same decision.

LY: Yes I did, and actually, I didn't make that decision. It was made for me and I will tell you what I'm talking about. Back at the end of the 1965 season the Astros were going to field the youngest team ever in the major leagues. I was going to be the oldest starting pitcher, at the age of twenty-one. Of course, given the fact that this was going to be the youngest team and everything else, it caught the eye of the newspapers, and lo and behold there was a quarter of a page article in *The New York Times*. I was really proud of it when I heard about it except the next thing I know my phone is ringing. My parents had read the article stating when the game was going to take place and that I was going to be the pitcher. I pick up the phone and it is my mother and she is saying (mimicking his mother's voice), "Larry, how can you do this to us?" "Mom, what are you talking about?" "You're embarrassing us. How can you pitch on Yom Kippur?" "Mom, I didn't know it and I promise you I will take care of it." Well, the next day I go to the ballpark and Paul Richards is walking around, he's the general manager, and I walk up to him and I tell him that my parents just called me and reminded me that it was Yom Kippur, that I had forgotten about it and that I'm going to have to back out. I apologized that I wasn't going to be able to pitch that game. He turned around and started apologizing to me profusely, "I'm sorry, I didn't know that." This made me feel a little better. But still, deep down in my heart, I think I really wanted to pitch that game, but it turned out that I just didn't. I decided not to pitch it and I listened to my parents. When my kids heard that story, especially my daughter Stacy, she was saying to me (mimicking his daughter's voice), "Dad, I didn't know that parents had such influence on their kids in those days. If you ever told me not to pitch on Yom Kippur, I would say that's my decision, not yours." So, we know there's been a change in the generations here, hasn't there?

Did it mean anything to you at the time to be one of the few Jewish guys playing professional baseball?

LY: You know the funny part of being Jewish, even back then, I never even thought about it. I didn't say to myself, "Hey, you know, I'm really good, not only as a player but I'm a Jewish boy who made it to the big leagues." I never said that to myself. I never looked at it that way. It was funny, a lot of other people did and I was very proud of it, but it just never sunk in in that manner to me.

You reached a point that you realized your baseball career was coming to an end and it's time to move on to something else. How is it that your baseball career winds down?

LY: Well, it winds down in 1965. I started the year, broke spring training and went to Oklahoma City and didn't do real well there. Then I went back to Amarillo, this time in the Texas League, given that I was in San Antonio the first time. First time I did pretty well there but the second time, nothing really to be proven. I didn't play all that great there either. Added to the fact that the mother of my children was pregnant with our son and undergoing some discomfort for the last six months of the pregnancy, coupled with the fact that I did not have the greatest season, I just decided to hang it up. Pure and simple. Have I regretted it looking back, retiring at the ripe old age of twenty-two? Yes. Is there anything I can do about it? No, but it does weigh on my mind every once in a while, but that's exactly what happened.

"They introduced me saying 'Designated Hitter, New York Yankees, Ron Blomberg.' I never knew what it was. I just went up there and hit."

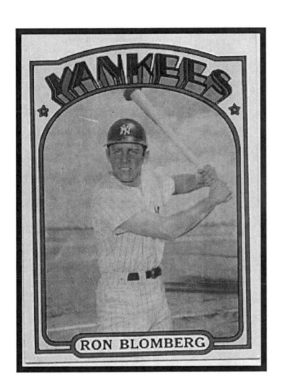

RON BLOMBERG

Best known for being Major League Baseball's first Designated Hitter, **Ron Blomberg** *burst onto the baseball scene in 1967 when he was baseball's and the New York Yankees' overall top pick in the annual amateur draft. Blomberg, from Atlanta, attended Druid Hills High School and graduated in 1967. He was not only a star baseball player, but also an all-star on both the basketball court and the football field. No other high school athlete has been chosen to the Parade All-America teams in football, basketball, and baseball. On the diamond he was known as a powerful left-handed hitter with a less than average glove. Bothered by nagging injuries throughout most of his career, he peaked in 1973 when he played in 100 games and hit a career best .329. It was opening day in 1973 at Fenway Park in Boston when Blomberg stepped up to the plate as the first DH. Facing Red Sox pitcher Luis Tiant, Blomberg walked to first base and into baseball history. Blomberg is known to joke that he was baseball's first DH, a "Designated Hebrew" that is. He finished his career with the Chicago White Sox in 1978. He was a career .293 hitter with 52 home runs and 224 RBI's. He scored 184 runs, had 67 doubles, and 8 triples in 461 total games.*

Blomberg lives in Roswell, Georgia and continues to stay active in baseball. He tutors young ballplayers to improve their hitting techniques. He also continues to participate in the New York Yankee fantasy camps held each off-season at the Yankees spring training complex in Tampa. Blomberg was inducted into the National Jewish Sports Hall of Fame in 2004. In 2006, Blomberg, along with Dan Schlossberg, wrote the book, Designated Hebrew: The Ron Blomberg Story. *In the summer of 2007, Blomberg managed the Bet Shemesh Blue Sox in the Israel Baseball League.*

What was it like growing up in Atlanta during the late 1950's and early 1960's? Were you were very involved in sports during that time?

RB: When I was growing up, the anti-Semitism, the John Birch Society, they were all a big part of the time in those days. But I basically never let that bother me. A lot of my teammates, where I went to high school, were members of the KKK and on Friday nights when they had their cross burnings, some of the guys had their hoods and their robes in their cars to go out to do their thing. It was very, very difficult but I never let it bother me. I knew it was there. I knew that people did not like Jews or they did not know much about them, so it was a difficult time. But, you know, I went through it and I made the best of it. Even to this day, I see some of the guys who were in the KKK or my friends who I grew up with, and to be honest with you, they didn't even know why they got involved in it. It was just like a family situation.

While you were playing in high school, was it a goal of yours to make it to the major leagues?

RB: Yes, at the age of eight or nine years old I knew I wanted to play Major League baseball, I guess because, at that time, when I went to grammar school, the New York Yankees were the big team down in Atlanta, and they always had them on the Saturday TV game of the week. I always looked at that as a fantasy to be able to play for the New York Yankees and to play Major League baseball.

So you're in high school and you are a very good player. When did you start to realize that you might have an opportunity to play in the major leagues?

RB: Well, I don't think I knew I had a shot. I guess I kept on improving, and my athletic ability took care of itself. I had my first encounter with a scout, a Braves scout by the name of Bob "Poochie" Hartsfield, and I had him out at one of my baseball games when I was in the ninth grade. He always told me to study hard and to play baseball and that maybe one day I would have the opportunity to play. I always kept that in the back of my mind. I knew that maybe I had the ability, but I kept on improving every single year, and then that ultimate moment came in 1967 when I was drafted by the New York Yankees.

You were a pretty good basketball player in high school too, correct?

RB: I was. I had almost a hundred basketball scholarship offers and almost seventy-five football scholarship offers. I had more football and basketball scholarship offers than baseball because baseball, back then, was not a big sport. The schools offering baseball scholarships were Florida, Florida State, UCLA, and teams like that. Basketball was a love of mine. I love all sports. I was pretty good in basketball. It was fun but you couldn't see a six-foot tall center playing college basketball. I had close to a 4-inch vertical leap at that particular time, so I knew that if I had an opportunity to play for a Major League team rather than basketball, where I could not have played in the NBA or the CBA or whatever, I knew that I was going to choose baseball.

How did your parents react when you let it be known that your career goal was to play professional baseball?

RB: Well, I always told my parents that I wanted to be a Major League Baseball player. It's just like you live in a fantasy and my parents said, "Oh yeah, you know, just enjoy the game of baseball and whatever happens, happens." They never pushed me into athletics. I had the fortunate ability to be a good athlete and my parents always let me do whatever I wanted to do. School work was number one and sports supposed to be was number two, but unfortunately, I took it the opposite way. I had sports number one and school work number two. My parents were a great influence on me in that they let me do what I wanted to do; they did not push me. When all the scouts came knocking at my door, when I was at the age of 15 or 16, when I started getting looked at quite a bit, it was an exciting time, but I never allowed it to take away from my school work so, basically, my parents left me to do anything I wanted to do.

When you were growing up, were there any professional Jewish athletes that you followed or looked up to as a role model?

RB: Well, I think that the major person when I was growing up was Sandy Koufax. Even to this day. I met Sandy maybe two or three times and he is a wonderful guy. But there were not really too many Jewish athletes when I played. Even when I went to high school, I may have had one or two other Jewish kids who were athletes in the whole school. At that particular time, the Jewish friends I grew up with really did not play many sports. Basically, what they did was to go to private schools, which I did not. They helped their parents in their own businesses; they wanted to become doctors or lawyers or inherit mom and dad's businesses. I was never like that. I was always a person who wanted to do my own thing. I wanted to play Major League Baseball and people looked at that and said, "Oh yeah, he's going to play Major League Baseball." But, you know, I fooled them and I had the opportunity, and to this day, the friends that I grew up with always talk about how they followed my career and were a fan.

You were the overall number one draft pick, by the New York Yankees, in the 1967 Major League Baseball draft. How much to you remember about that day?

RB: I remember that day very well. It was the day of my graduation when I got drafted number one. It was on the UPI and AP wires, on the cover of a lot of newspapers across the country. Especially getting drafted by the New York Yankees and how big the Jewish population is in New York, even though I had not signed yet, I must have had so many people find my number and they contacted me, people who were Yankee fans who wanted to wish me the best and wanted me to sign with the Yankees. It was almost like I was their Messiah. If I had an opportunity, I wanted to play for the New York Yankees, stay with the

Jewish people up in New York, and be like an idol to all the Jewish kids, to say that if you have the ability, a Jewish person can follow his dreams and be whatever he or she wanted to be.

After being the number one selection in 1967, you spent a couple of seasons in the minor leagues. What was the pressure like for you once you finally made it to the big league club? And, at the same time, was there any pressure being a high profile Jewish athlete playing in New York?

RB: Well, you know, being a seventeen-year-old athlete when I got signed, I really didn't feel like I was under pressure. I enjoyed it. I guess that's why I did well in athletics. I did not let anything bother me. I just let things work themselves out and fortunately they did. When I had my first visit up to New York, they had a big sign for me on Seventh Avenue. I got to Yankee Stadium and there was Walter Cronkite and Phil Rizzuto. They interviewed me; it was a dream come true. There was no pressure. I think I felt like I was living in a fantasy world and I accomplished whatever I wanted to do. Now it was my turn to take it to another extreme and to do really well up in the big leagues.

Rooming with Mickey Mantle at spring training in 1968 must have been a thrill for you.

RB: I'm down at spring training, I'm eighteen years old. We're in Fort Lauderdale at a place called The Yankee Clipper. That's where all the old Yankees stayed when they were participating in spring training. They had me rooming with Mickey, although it wasn't actually rooming with him. I had adjoining rooms with Mickey, but I never saw him. The only thing I ever saw of Mickey's was his suitcases. He never used his room during spring training because of whatever reason. The only time I actually got to see Mickey was at the training table at the stadium. So, I did share an adjoining room with him, but he never came into his room. Mickey, however, became a very close friend of mine after many, many years.

In 1967, coming out of your first spring training, you're assigned to the Yankees Minor League team in Johnson City, Tennessee. Do you remember what it was like for you to head out on your first professional baseball assignment?

RB: You know, you anticipate a variety of situations but I was very, very lucky. I had a cousin who was the president of the Johnson City Yankees and also he was also a real big merchant in Johnson City, Tennessee, where they actually took good care of me. When you're seventeen years old, signing professionally and making a few dollars, traveling by buses, meeting new people, a lot of Hispanics, blacks, whites, all different types of people, you have to make friends with them. You know, they become brothers of yours. Johnson City was a great little town and they really took great care of us.

From Johnson City you moved up to Manchester, New Hampshire. What was that transition like for you?

RB: Yes, Manchester was Double-A and I was up at Double-A for two and a half months. I made the All-Star team while at Manchester and then, following that, I got called up to the Yankees for, I think, thirty days. It was one of those late season call-ups in September. I did real well while I was up with the Yankees. At that time, they wanted me to go to Syracuse so I went to Syracuse for a year. I had a good year. I was the youngest guy, I think, in the International League. I was going on nineteen years old and hitting extremely well. At that time the Yankees stunk, and they needed someone who was fairly popular. The Jewish population was really, really big and kept them talking about me coming up. Once I made it back up, from that day on I stayed in the bigs and I stayed with the Yankees.

Do you remember what it was like and what you were feeling that first time you were called up to the major leagues?

RB: Well, I was eighteen years old and being able to play with all the big boys, especially at Yankee Stadium, where Mickey Mantle, Joe DiMaggio, Lou Gehrig and Babe Ruth and Casey Stengel, you know, all the great stars had been and being able to participate in a forum where anybody would just die to be, it was the greatest.

Do you remember your first at-bat against the Detroit Tigers in September of 1969?

RB: The first at-bat I ever had was against Joe Coleman, and I walked. The second at-bat that I had against Detroit, and I hit a home run. So, the first time I walked, the second time I hit a home run.

During your time with the Yankees, you played for a few managers, but the two that stand out would have to be Ralph Houk and, of course, Billy Martin.

RB: I did. To be honest with you, I thought Ralph Houk was probably the best field manager that I actually ever had. That's why they called him "The Major." Billy Martin was a different breed. The few years that I had him, he went back and forth from the Yankees, getting fired and rehired three or four times. But, the best staff was when I came up. It was Ralph Houk, Elston Howard, Whitey Ford, Yogi Berra, and Jim Turner, who was the pitching coach. We had some great baseball minds. Unfortunately, we didn't have the quickest of teams, but we started growing and we started really improving an awful lot when George Steinbrenner came in. He bought the team from CBS, and he really inundated the Yankees with a lot of money and new players through free-agency.

Do you remember experiencing a feeling of pride in that you were, at that time, one of the few active Jewish players to be in the major leagues?

RB: Oh absolutely. I think if I played in Kansas City or Detroit, it would have been a lot different than playing in New York. You have got to be a special person to be able to be an athlete up in New York, especially with a person that had the recognition that I did, being a Jewish athlete. The whole town is basically run by Jews, from the garment district to the restaurants, to all the people up around that area. They looked at me as somebody they could feel good about. To say, "Here's a Jewish athlete, that my son wants to be in the major leagues, he's not doing well in school." Well, I could talk to the kid and let him know that he could reach his goal but that you've got to do real well in school. I think I had a nice career up in New York with the Yankees, but unfortunately I got injured quite a bit. I still had a great career recognition-wise and the fans have always been great to me. I did some TV and radio work up there. I've been able to work with some great people like Phil Rizzuto, Marv Albert, Murray "the K" Kaufman, and John Sterling and enjoy being able to be part of New York City. Being part of New York is the greatest thing in the world. When I go up there I feel like that's "My City." It's a city where I did well and made a lot of friends so I would say that playing in New York was the greatest thing I could have accomplished in my baseball career.

So you're a young Jewish guy in New York and playing with the Yankees. Were there any special perks that came along with being in your position?

RB: Well, I think so. I don't think I ever paid for a car, eating in a restaurant, and to this day I go up there for Old-Timers' Day and my picture is still hanging up in the Stage Deli, in Carnegie's Deli and places like that in the city. Wherever I go, it's really funny, I haven't played baseball in twenty-five, thirty years or whatever, but every time I make a dinner reservation up there I'll start by saying, "This is Ron Blomberg," and the first thing they say, if they don't remember me as a former Yankee, is to ask if I am related to the mayor up there. It's really fun up there. I also met a lot of people while I was up there, from the wealthiest to the poorest, from Frank Sinatra to Jay Black with Jay and the Americans, the Rockettes. I did all the stuff with Walter Cronkite. I was on the Johnny Carson Show, I was on the David Letterman Show, the Dick Cavett Show. It was a thrill in my lifetime to be able to see all of those things and to be a part of those things and to be well respected up there, even to this day.

We've all heard the stories of Sandy Koufax and Hank Greenberg not playing on the high Jewish holidays. Did you ever come across a situation where you had to make a similar decision?

RB: Yes, sure. It was in 1973. It was funny too. I was hitting around .350 or .360 and we were just coming off a series with the Cleveland Indians. Rosh Hashanah was the next day. Most everybody knew, maybe not the coaches, that it was the next day and I told them that I could not play baseball on Rosh Hashanah or Yom Kippur. That was one of the points that I made early on. Even the day I signed, they asked me at that particular time if I played on Rosh Hashanah or Yom Kippur and I said absolutely not. I did sit out for both.

I'm guessing that because you were in New York and not Kansas City or Cleveland that you were under some pressure and the microscope per se, to not play on the Jewish holidays.

RB: It was magnified but still, that was my belief. Even if I had been in Kansas City, I would not have played on Rosh Hashanah or Yom Kippur. If I had played during the High Holidays in New York, I think they would have burned me in effigy and I would have been destroyed. I didn't play and that was my belief and what I wanted to do.

Did you ever face any verbal abuse or hear any anti-Semitic comments during your baseball career be it in the minors or the majors?

RB: Well, not really, not player wise. When I was in the minor leagues after I first signed, I would go up to these small country towns back then and they would always write articles about me being the Yankees' first draft pick. I had a few people would say stuff like, "Here's the Jew ballplayer," but that was about it. I would hear things, but no one would ever come up and say anything to my face.

Did you ever play with any other Jewish players while you were in New York?

RB: Yes, I did. Elliott Maddox, who had converted to Judaism, was one. There was Kenny Holtzman, who I played with on the Yankees and who had come over from Oakland. Art Shamsky, who was playing for the New York Mets at the time; he and I also became very good friends.

You also played with a lot of great players, Reggie Jackson being one of them. What was it like to be a teammate of his?

RB: Reggie was a different individual. You know, he floated his own boat. He always got along extremely well with me. Reggie was the type of person that wanted the limelight on himself all the time. There's nothing wrong with that if you can back up your words. He did back up his words, but unfortunately, he alienated a lot of his teammates even to this day. When he was out on the baseball field, he produced. You have to give him a hundred and ten percent credit. Like I said before, Reggie was always very nice to me. Even to this day he'll go out of his way to talk to me. I always liked Reggie, but he was a different type of guy. That's why back in the 1970's they called the Yankees the "Bronx Zoo," because we had so many different personalities on that team.

You will forever be remembered as Major League Baseball's first ever Designated Hitter. Tell me about that day and what you remember most about it.

RB: Well, it was just a normal day. At that time, in 1973, they put the DH rule in because they wanted some more publicity and increased attendance. It was a major pinch-hitters role is basically what it was. I was down in spring training and I had pulled a hamstring. We had a DH on our team but I never really paid it too much attention. I was on the flight back to New York once camp broke, and Ralph Houk came up to me asked me if I would be the DH for the opening series in Boston. He asked me if I could hit four times. I said "yes." So I got to the ballpark in Boston and saw my name on the lineup card as being the DH. I didn't have any idea what to do. Elston Howard and Dick Howser were our coaches, and I asked them, "What do I do?" He said to just go up there and take batting practice, don't take any fielding practice. So, the day of the game, in Boston against Luis Tiant, they introduced me saying, "Designated Hitter, New York Yankees, Ron Blomberg." I never knew what it was. I just went up there and hit. We lost the game 15-5. Mel Stottlemyre lost the game to Luis Tiant. After the game I got back into the clubhouse and there were something like 75 to 80 reporters around me. They are telling me that I made baseball history as the first Major League Baseball Designated Hitter. Marty Appell, our public relations guy, took my bat and some pictures and sent them to the Hall of Fame. So, I became known as the first DH. I never thought it would stay in baseball, but now it's thirty years later and I became a legend in the game of baseball. They can never take it away from me. Every time they talk about the DH in the World Series or the All-Star game they always bring me up. So, it's really been a nice go around.

How cool is it to know that your bat, the one you used in that first Designated Hitter at-bat, is in the Baseball Hall of Fame in Cooperstown?

RB: Well, it's great. I think the toughest thing is that I did not fulfill the potential that I had because of the injuries. I was very injury-prone and at that time, there was not the modern medical technology that players today receive once they get injured. Essentially, they just didn't have that that technology to really spring me back to one hundred percent. Just getting to Yankee Stadium and getting at-bats with fifty thousand people standing up for you and cheering you, I mean, that's the place of all places. The New Yorkers are the greatest fans in the whole world. I feel so much a part of that whenever I go back to New York.

Did you used to draw a Star of David on the end of your bats?

RB: I did. I put a Star of David with one less point. The one reason why I put one less point is because I had not yet become a true baseball "star." If I had ever become that, I would have put a real Jewish star on it. People didn't know that, they looked at the star and thought it was the Star of David. It was actually a semi-

Star of David, with one less point because I did not become the major star that I wanted to be.

As a former Yankee, you've got to be a little sad to see the end of the line for Yankee Stadium as they move into a new facility.

RB: I think the "House that Ruth Built," what they called Yankee Stadium, is by far the greatest stadium that I've ever been involved in. Unfortunately, they've closed it down and I have a lot of mixed emotions. I understand that they are going to be moving to a new ball park across the street because of financial reasons. It's going to be state of the art, like something from another universe. I know all of these other new stadiums are beautiful and whatever, but nothing can compare to the Yankees and what they do. Yankee Stadium is to me, because I played up in New York, by far the greatest stadium I ever played in.

Only handful of teams—the Yankees, Red Sox, Cubs, and Dodgers—have the kind of lengthy history that makes franchises special, whether as a player or a fan. In the case of the Yankees, what was it for you that made it so special to be a part of?

RB: Ownership. There are two types of players up in New York. You produce or you don't produce. They like you or they don't like you. There's no in-between with Yankee fans. You give them a hundred and twenty percent and they'll boo you still, but they respect you more than anything in the whole world. They have given so many athletes five, six, seven or more chances, just like a Darryl Strawberry or a Dwight Gooden or Steve Howe, people like that. The fans are a very key aspect of New York athletes and it means so much.

"I'm fond of what I did. I made the right choice. But I definitely feel, you might say, that I was in a position to catch hell for it. If one prejudice doesn't get me, the other one will."

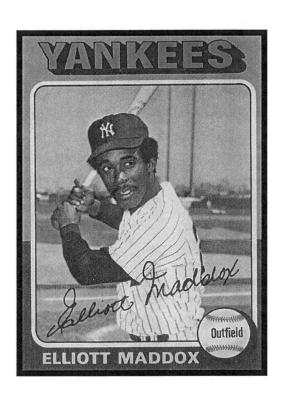

ELLIOTT MADDOX

Elliott Maddox *was born in East Orange, New Jersey. An outstanding baseball player at Union County High School and later at the University of Michigan, where he won the 1968 Big Ten Conference batting title with a .467 average, Maddox was a first-round draft pick by the Detroit Tigers in 1968. After just two seasons in the minor leagues, in Lakeland, Florida and Rocky Mount, North Carolina, he made his big league debut when the Tigers offered him a contract in 1970. During his eleven-year career, Maddox played for the Detroit Tigers, Washington Senators, Texas Rangers, New York Yankees, Baltimore Orioles, and New York Mets. Maddox enjoyed his most productive season while with the Yankees in 1974 when he led the team, hitting .303 with 141 hits and 69 walks in 137 games. He played with the Yankees in the 1976 World Series. Maddox made the decision to convert to Judaism in 1975.*

One little-known interesting side note is that Maddox played for the legendary and fiery Billy Martin with three different teams: the Tigers, Rangers, and Yankees. While with each of those teams Martin had him traded. In 1971 he went from the Tigers to the Rangers, in 1974 from the Rangers to the Yankees, and in 1976 from the Yankees to the Orioles. He played his final game with the Mets on October 1, 1980, finishing with his career average of .261 with 18 home runs and 234 RBI's. He returned to the Yankees in 1990 and 1991, serving as a bench coach under manager Buck Showalter. In 2007, Maddox was inducted into the Hall of Fame in his hometown of Union County, New Jersey. He now lives in South Florida.

Elliott, can you tell me a little bit about your upbringing and your early road to a career in professional baseball.

EM: Well, I was born and raised in northeast New Jersey, not far from New York City, about twelve or thirteen miles from New York. I had an older brother and a younger sister, so I was the proverbial middle child. I was the sickly one as a kid, at a young age. My brother participated in sports. I remember when I turned eight I wanted to play Little League, but I couldn't because I was sick at the time. The doctors said that I would have to wait at least a year so I played when I was nine. I actually did very well. At that time, Little League was for kids ages eight through twelve, pretty much playing together if you were good enough to make it so I was on the so-called "Major League" team at nine. I played in all sports in junior high, ran track and cross-county, played baseball and basketball, football, you name it. In high school I even added soccer. The area that I grew up in was a mixed area, mixed meaning not just black, white, Puerto Rican, but also German and Italian. Yet, my closest friends in the immediate area were predominantly black and in school my closest friends were either black or Jewish. After high school I went off to the University of Michigan, from where I ultimately graduated, but it was back in the ninth grade that a teacher, an English teacher, for an assignment told us to write out what we planned to do with our lives after college. At that time I said that I was going to play Major League Baseball for approximately eight years and then become a professional, and I said, "Hopefully a doctor." When I started at Michigan I was in pre-med. The ironic thing about that was that I planned on being a Major League ballplayer. There was no ands, ifs or buts about it. It wasn't that I hoped to be a Major League player, as I said, I hoped to be a doctor. It was just always part of my life plan, just like when you wake up in the morning, you're breathing or when you are tired, you get some sleep. I planned to be a ballplayer and fortunately that's the way it happened. I was drafted out of high school in the third round by the Houston Astros. I didn't sign. I played at Michigan and signed as the eleventh player picked in the country in the first round by the Detroit Tigers. I eventually graduated, but it took me a little longer because I would only go to school during the winter at that point. By the end of my junior year, I was playing Major League baseball.

Tell me about your first baseball coach, a gentleman by the name of Mark Shapiro. I understand that he had an early influence on you.

EM: Yes, Mark Shapiro was my first Little League coach. I don't know if he planned on being a role model and such and I don't know if I would call him a role model or a major influence aside from the fact that he was my first coach. There were some other people who influenced me, an attorney and a politician in my town, Union, New Jersey, who was the mayor. His name was Anthony Russo. Now he had an influence on my life, which was tremendous. I came to know him because both of my parents were involved in local politics. Possibly the only person who I idolized was my maternal grandfather, the only grandparent of mine that I ever knew. He was a hard worker and a great family man and he was definitely special to me.

After spending just two seasons in the minor leagues in Florida and North Carolina, you joined the Detroit Tigers for the 1970 season. However, you were only there for that one year before getting traded to the Washington Senators. The Senators, following the 1971 season moved to Arlington and became the Texas Rangers. How did that trade come about so early in your career and what was it like to now be playing in Texas?

EM: Texas back in 1972-73 when I was there, that was the first time they had Major League Baseball, and it was football country so it wasn't a place for baseball players; it wasn't a place for blacks; and it wasn't a place for Jews. They called it the great Southwest, but the mentality was that it was simply part of the South. I was never comfortable there, definitely at the end of 1973. When I was in Detroit, Billy Martin became the manager there and it was Billy who had me traded to the Washington Senators. Three years later Billy was fired in Detroit and became the manager of the Rangers. He and I just never saw eye-to-eye, so that just added to the frustrations. After three weeks, he got there in September of 1973, and three weeks later, right at the end of the season, I was traded to the Yankees. When I came back home I was comfortable and I could go back into my normal routine. I had time to go out and do things so that was the time for me to go through the conversion.

The conversion you refer to took place in 1975. It was a life-altering decision. You decided to convert to Judaism. What prompted you to make this decision?

EM: If there was a time that I could say it started, it was in high school with a friend, someone who was in my home room named Ron Meyer. I would see Ronnie every day, Monday through Friday, before classes started and after classes ended. Ronnie should have been a rabbi actually, but he would talk to me every day about Judaism and Judaism versus Christianity and why he would do this I had no idea. He wasn't Orthodox, and then again, the Orthodox probably weren't about to talk to me anyway, but Ronnie would just tell me things about the Jewish faith and I had personally had some reservations about a few things in Christianity, which I'm not really going to get into. There were just a lot of things I didn't like. I was always a history buff and it used to bother me, like going back to when we studied the Crusades as a young person in school and you had the crusaders from Europe going into Asia Minor telling people, "You've got to believe this and you've got to believe that or we're going to kill you." I just had big problems with it. At Michigan I was fortunate enough, after I signed my baseball contract, to switch my major and I double-majored in history and political science. With history Michigan offered many courses such as Judaic History and History of Islam and so on and so forth. I didn't want to take the run-of-the-mill courses so I studied Judaic History. I actually found out, and remember that this was back in the late 60's, the civil rights movement was going on, the Vietnam War was going. Judaism coincided with what I already believed in. The history of blacks throughout the world, particularly in the Western world, the United States, so resembled the history of the Jewish people that I said, "This is definitely for me." I can't say that I changed my faith or my beliefs. I simply gave my beliefs a religion, a named religion.

What was that like, to be back in New York, to be a well known athlete playing for the Yankees, to approach a rabbi in a synagogue and request a conversion to Judaism?

EM: Being that I wasn't doing it in Williamsburg, I think it helped a little bit. The rabbi recognized who I was. That basically was it. There were no problems. Orthodox Judaism you can't convert into, you can't go through the conversion process and Reform, you are not going to learn anything so with a Conservative rabbi it worked out very nicely. There were no problems with the congregation, it was fantastic.

The fact that you were a Major League Baseball player, did the community open its arms to you even more so because of that?

EM: I can't say if it was because I was a ballplayer or not because I never had any problems. Not everyone knew that I played ball. I never had any problems with those individuals or with the ones who knew I was a ballplayer.

Was it well known in the latter stages of your career that you had converted? Was it known by the other players around Major League baseball?

EM: It was known.

Did you ever get any feedback regarding your conversion, positive or negative, from any other players when you were with the Orioles or the Mets?

EM: From other players, no. There were some things from management that were definitely based on, what shall we say, prejudice.

You mentioned that you recognized a number of similarities between the two, between black history and the history of the Jewish people.

EM: Yes, there is definitely a kindred spirit there, and as a matter of fact I still study whenever possible. I go online and read things. I want to go to Egypt now, Southern Egypt to be specific, and to northern Sudan to the area known as Nubia, which is where the blacks originated. They then went off to Ethiopia and so on and so forth. But Judaism had its roots in Ethiopia with blacks there and it's funny because I have a lot of people who ask, "Jeez, I've never seen a black Jew before." I tell them, "You just haven't been looking because there are plenty."

Wasn't there some speculation that so-called "Lost Tribe," the thirteenth tribe, was a tribe of black Jews?

EM: That's right. You can't tell by our profile. The noses are a little different. I've never had anyone say to me as I'm walking down the street, "Hey, look at that

list." One of her brothers looks over at me, and you could see the embarrassment on his face. Finally he says to them, as I was walking away from the table, "Hey, you know Elliott's Jewish and I think you guys have gone too far already. You'd better stop." That was something, but that was the South and unfortunately it's just the way some people are.

How religiously active are you as a Reform Jew?

EM: When you say religious, I have my thoughts on religion and on Judaism and, of course I don't adhere to everything in the Jewish religion or Jewish culture. But, I consider myself very religious. I don't feel I have to go and sit with the congregation in a building to communicate with God or to observe the laws, so I don't attend temple very often. I go more than just on the High Holy Days, but am I there every week or am I there twice a month? No. Do I fast? Yes. I mean there were a couple of times during my career where there were games played on Yom Kippur, which I did not participate in.

That was actually going to be my next question, regarding whether or not you played during the Jewish High Holy Days. You were an everyday player, so the chances were good that you were going to face that situation, whereas a pitcher might not be affected at all.

EM: Oh yes, with a pitcher, the other guys on the team may not even notice that he's not there on that particular day but if you are an everyday player, and you just don't show up, it's like "What the hell happened? Where is he?" But as I stated earlier, everyone knew, so it was no problem. I remember Joe Torre saying to me about a week before the holiday, when I was on the Mets and he was the manager. He and I were friends even before I came to the Mets as a free agent. The reason I came was two-fold, it was coming back home and also because Joe was the manager and we had such a good relationship. And he said, "Okay, I see Yom Kippur is coming up, so I know you won't be here." That was so nice to hear. I mean that was great. You may wonder why I appreciated that so much. It's because here was a fellow player, a manager who simply respected me as a man with my religion and there were no problems about it. He was making plans for me not to be there. You didn't get that very often from people higher up in management. It was rare as a matter of fact.

What are you involved with these days?

EM: Well, my son, who I've been raising as a single parent, recently went off to college. I took him off to college at the University of South Florida so I'm trying to remember now what it's like to have a life again because when I got full custody of him, I had been counseling teenagers. Kids like what they term "end-of-the-road kids," kids that were pretty tough adolescents, just about all with criminal records.

I had cases directed my way by the court system. But when I got full custody I actually gave that up; I stopped doing everything. I opened a baseball school here in Coral Springs, Florida but that is part-time. I gave up all full-time endeavors so that I could be there for my son, to be the parent who was making breakfast in the morning and then to be there in the afternoon when he came home so on and so forth. I'll get back into the work force so to speak. I am putting a fantasy camp together, which is going to be outstanding. It's actually former New York Mets and New York Yankees players participating.

Do you have any thoughts or desires to coach at the Minor League or Major League level?

EM: No. I would like to work in a front office, and by that I don't mean be a general manager or president of a team. Some type of scouting would be good or I would absolutely adore public relations or community relations. That would be fantastic.

"I went into the game and got my first at-bat against Nolan Ryan, which was very exciting. I closed my eyes, swung the bat, and happened to hit a hard ground ball to Dickie Thon at short."

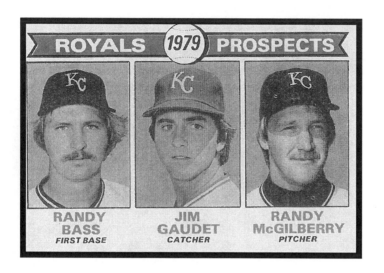

JIM GAUDET

Jim Gaudet

Jim Gaudet *experienced what in baseball is known as a "Cup of Coffee,"*
spending just a very short time in the major leagues. He played in a total of six
games over two seasons with the Kansas City Royals. He registered 14 at-bats,
his very first coming against Hall of Fame flame-thrower Nolan Ryan. His
only hit came in 1979 against another Hall of Fame pitcher, Rich "Goose"
Gossage. The New Orleans native played college baseball at Tulane University.
He was first drafted in June of 1973, taken by the Atlanta Braves in the third
round of the amateur draft. He did not sign, instead choosing to remain in
college. He was later drafted by the Royals in the sixth round of the 1976 draft.
In the minor leagues he spent time in Evansville, Indiana and Omaha,
Nebraska. His final Major League appearance was on September 30, 1979. He
is now a chiropractor in Macon, Georgia.

Can you tell me a little bit about your background in baseball, both in college and the pros? You
were not in the major leagues that long, but you did spend time in both the Royals and Blue Jays
organizations.

JG: Well, I was drafted by the Atlanta Braves when I was still in high school but
decided not to sign with them at the time and went to play baseball at Tulane
University on a scholarship there. I've recently been informed that my years at
Tulane, I think, were the last time a baseball full-ride scholarship was given. Now
they are all like partials or percentages for college players. From Tulane, after my
junior year, I was drafted in the sixth round by the Kansas City Royals as a catcher
and began my first season in rookie camp and then was moved up to Double-A by
the end of the first season with the Jacksonville Suns. The next year, in 1977, I
played in Jacksonville, Florida for a full season and from 1978 through 1982 was in
Omaha, Nebraska, the Triple-A affiliate of the Royals, and in Kansas City for
September call-ups in 1978 and 1979 and broke with the club in 1980. After that I
was sent back down to Evansville, Indiana and then later played in Omaha again.
My last season was spent with the Toronto Blue Jays organization in Syracuse,
New York. I was released in May and that is basically my baseball story.

Is it safe to assume that like most young kids who enjoy playing baseball that you were trying to
live out your dream to play professional baseball?

JG: Basically, as a kid, we all have the childhood dreams of being a Major League
baseball player. At an early age I was blessed with the natural ability to play sports.

I lettered in four sports in high school. In New Orleans at a pretty prestigious Catholic high school call Jesuit High School, I played football, basketball, ran track and high jumped, and also played baseball, but of all the sports baseball was by far my favorite. It came very easy to me although it took a lot of hard work, especially as you get into the high school ranks. It's interesting because when you're blessed with skills like that—well, in hindsight, I guess in all respects, you took it for granted because you feel like, yes, it is my destination and I will stop at nothing to get there. It eventually did unfold. It happened in a storybook fashion for me in a sense, even though I just saw a little bit of the major leagues. I did have six years of professional baseball. I kind of felt that as a kid playing in Little League ball and high school ball that I was fortunate enough to have the athletic ability and honed in on the mental capacity to handle Major League baseball at the Minor League level and the Major League level.

You were in the Kansas City Royals organization from 1977 to 1979. There were a lot of good and a few great players with the Royals during those seasons. What was that like, being around those caliber players?

JG: To me, I got to play in the major leagues, being in pro ball from 1976 through 1982, especially the golden years as I called them for the Kansas City Royals, winning, I think, three or four division titles and the World Series in 1980. At that time they had the long-term contracts, like George Brett, Frank White, Paul Splittorff, John Mayberry, Dave Nelson, and Willie Wilson. The great coaches, managers like Whitey Herzog. You still see them around baseball today, twenty-five some odd years later. So, to me it was short, but it was very powerful because I have so many little cameos or vignettes of things that happened to me. For instance, my first at bat in the major leagues was against Nolan Ryan. I had just been called up the day before, we had an off day and here I come out of the bullpen in the seventh inning, nervous as all get-out as you can imagine. I went into the game and got my first at-bat against Nolan Ryan, which was very exciting. Yes, of course, I closed my eyes, swung the bat, and happened to hit a hard ground ball to Dickie Thon at short, which bounced up. Rod Carew was on first. I get on first. Carew says to me, "You should have gotten a hit, kid." My only hit in the major leagues came in the 1979 season, at Yankee Stadium. It was a base hit off "Goose" Gossage. And so, there are very minimal highlights, a "cup of coffee and a bagel" if you will. Those were the golden years in pro ball, I think, and it's changed so much since then. We all have some kind of connection to baseball, and for me it fulfilled my childhood dream.

You mentioned that you were originally drafted by the Atlanta Braves in the third round in 1973 in the amateur draft but did not sign. What was the reasoning behind that decision? Was it because you had a full scholarship offer to attend Tulane University and wanted to go to college?

JG: No. You know, as an eighteen-year-old kid coming out of high school, I was itching to sign. I came up to the old Atlanta-Fulton County Stadium and stayed across the street at the International Hotel. I went to two workouts. Connie Ryan, I think, was the one who had scouted me and I was really interested in signing. It was a dream come true. It's very tough when they put you in a Major League uniform and on a Major League field, not to try and pursue your dream of playing Major League ball. But, basically, my father was trying to be sort of a helpful agent for me at the time. I played some all-star baseball traveling a lot around the country. In the summer of that year, I didn't think the money was enough at the time to compare it to an education at Tulane University, plus the opportunity to play baseball at Tulane. A funny thing happened. The night before I decided to go to Tulane, the night before I went to my first class, I got a call from the Atlanta Braves, and Connie Ryan said, "Jim, we'd like to make another offer to you and increase the value of the signing bonus." It may have ended up being $52,000 or $54,000 in 1973 and I don't know what that would equate to today. I'm sure third-round picks get a lot more than that nowadays. I did my own sort of study after three years at Tulane before I signed a professional baseball contract. Financially, the comparison study of what it would have cost me to go to Tulane, to go to the many places I was able to go to with Tulane playing summer ball, whether it was Hawaii or the Riverside tournament in Riverside, California, whether it was playing in Alaska in one of the more prestigious summer leagues in college ball plus the cost of tuition at Tulane, it was a very close comparison in that three years' time. Another factor was that coming out of Tulane as a junior, my first year in pro ball I went to Double-A. I would have started at the rookie level if I had been coming out of high school. I think it was a good decision for me to go to college, and I urge kids coming out of high school, that unless they're in those top rounds, I do think college should be the first choice.

So you've been through college, the minor leagues, and a couple of seasons in the majors with Kansas City. Your decision to convert to Judaism comes about because of what and of what faith were you prior to your conversion?

JG: I grew up in a Catholic family, attending parochial schools in New Orleans. I think growing up I had sort of an individuality that I felt I was different, not because of my baseball skills but from other different areas. I started to see things happen within the Catholic faith and in the Catholic religion. Growing up and going to the high school I went to, I started to have a different theological thought process, the idea of religion, the idea of spirituality. Adding influence to that would be my wife Jamie of twenty-nine years, who I met my junior year at Tulane, she was transferring from Springfield College in Massachusetts and she was a senior at Tulane. She was Jewish and a couple of ballplayers on the team were Jewish. I had hung out with a lot of kids in college who were Jewish and started to become more aligned with the behavior, the mindset and thought process and those types of relationships and communications and felt more comfortable in that atmosphere than I did around a lot of my friends growing up in high school. Fast forward, when I got to Tulane University, I realized that I had a hard time with a lot of the teachings and the tenets of the Catholic faith and religion. I did feel very strongly about the fact of one God and became very monotheistic. That sort of led me to pursue other possibilities of religion. I decided, probably in 1976 after I signed, that I was going to pursue other religions and certainly Judaism started to soar to the top of the list for a number of different reasons. It just basically fits my lifestyle, my belief in one God.

A very interesting turn of events, to say the least.

JG: My story is kind of different because here is somebody who is a Cajun Catholic who grows up to be a Jewish chiropractor. A lot of that is with the help, of course, with my wife Jamie, who has opened up a whole new world for me just being who she is and also allowing me to pursue and seek what I feel is comfortable in my spirituality and my theological preference. I think I have a better appreciation of Judaism because I've gone through Catholicism, which enables me to understand the "other side."

Coming from the Cajun country down in Louisiana, with your background, what was the response of your parents to your decision to convert?

JG: Well, my father really didn't understand it because his parents and his family were very, very devout Catholic. On the other hand, my mother, just sort of in a humorous way, said that "it's just great to see a prayer book in Jimmy's hand." Although they didn't understand it at first, I think they've come to understand a lot about how the likenesses of religions of Catholicism and Judaism are. They took it quite well. I think our family has understood our plight of building our own family and our own community in Macon, Georgia and I think they've appreciated how devout we are in our religion today.

Once you made the decision to convert to Judaism, what did you do to get the process started and what did the process entail?

JG: Well, I'm in Evansville, Indiana. We find a Conservative shul. We talked to the rabbi and I spent probably two weeks there when I was in town, a couple of hours each morning, learning a pretty strict format of what literature and/or books are to be read, discussions that took place during the process. You go through a learning process but it's a lot of interaction with the rabbi. After two to three weeks in Evansville with a Conservative rabbi, I shift to Omaha and it continues with a Reform rabbi. This rabbi does not demand as much but did go through about a month-long process of readings and teachings and finally signed the document into reformed, and there is a position of denouncing the previous religion, which to me wasn't that difficult. Technically, with the rabbi's blessing and a few documents here and there, I converted into Reform Judaism in 1980. However, when we got to Macon and were accepted by the Conservative synagogue, up until the new rabbi came around twelve years ago, there was a just a little technical glitch, and for the Conservative conversion, I basically had to go through a little bit more of intense study and then the official Mikvah, for which I had to come up to Atlanta and have two other rabbis for the three rabbis to witness, the conversion processes, the documents and the Mikvah and basically finalize the exclamation point at the end of the classification of Conservative Jewry.

An interesting tidbit to your story involves your agent during your later years, someone who really had a first-hand look at being Jewish and playing baseball.

JG: Yes, my agent happened to have been Steve Greenberg, Hank Greenberg's son. In my later years, 1978 to 1982, it was very interesting having seen *The Hank Greenberg Story*. To go back and look at the evolution of the Jewish player, whether that movie truly depicted Hank Greenberg or not, it definitely gave you an appreciation for sitting out on Yom Kippur and to me it's a tough call. We have not allowed our children to play sports events on Yom Kippur. As a matter of fact, my son played soccer here and there is a couple of other players on the team that were Jewish and missed a practice on Yom Kippur and the very next night they were benched for the whole first half of the soccer game and so they, henceforth, were known as the "Day of Atonement Twins."

You had an interesting situation arise one time when you were with the Royals. Tell me about that.

JG: I think it was in 1979 when I was with the Royals, while we were down in spring training. Amos Otis played for the Royals and he used to have a swastika on the bottom of his bat. He used these wooden bats that did not have a knob on the bottom but he put that swastika on it. It offended me enough to say to him, "You need to take that off the bottom of your bat. Some people would find that very offensive." He was ignorant to the fact that he really didn't know what it meant. He put it on there to be able to see his bat in the bat rack among all of the other numbered bats. Not too long after that, it must have been six to eight weeks later, he was in Chicago playing the White Sox and the same issue was brought back to his attention. John Schuerholtz called him into his office and told him that he was not to put that sign on his bat ever again. He didn't know or was not aware of other religions or teachings. I found it odd that he was not aware of the Holocaust. That was really an interesting episode that kind of rubbed me the wrong way. I'm glad it was rectified, but I did not really see too many negative instances. It was early then, the late seventies, early eighties and you're seeing more and more of a Jewish baseball player who, I'm sure is very proud to be Jewish. I think there is more ignorance than there is direct assault on somebody because they're Jewish. You still see some anti-Semitism and you'll see it some in sports, but I think it is downplayed to the point where I think more people and players have respect for each other. There is so much of an influx of international players, everywhere from Panama to the Dominican Republic to Mexico to Japan. What happens to the Japanese players now? Is it Buddhist religion that they believe in? So, I don't think that religion comes much into play in baseball.

What brought about the end of your career in baseball?

JG: I think I was twenty-five years old and I tore my left knee ligament, my ACL, playing in the Dominican Republic in the winter leagues. I knew at that point in time that it was either going to be a long standing rehab to come back and the technology for ligament replacement was antiquated compared to the medical technology of today for ACL. I played with it torn for about a year and a half and started to think that it was time to move on. I got out of the game in 1982 and went back to two years of undergraduate science requirement study after I'd gone the three years at Tulane University so five years of undergraduate study and the four years of chiropractic college and that's where I am today. I'm in Macon, Georgia, where I've been a practicing chiropractor for twenty years now.

*"I had never even met a Major League Baseball player.
Actually the first Major League game that I ever went to
was the first one I played in."*

RICHIE
SCHEINBLUM
KANSAS CITY ROYALS   OUTFIELD

RICHIE SCHEINBLUM

Richie Scheinblum *rose up from an early childhood of foster homes all the way to a Major League Baseball career that saw him spend time with six different teams. Growing up in the South Bronx, Scheinblum excelled in a number of different sports, especially baseball. He received a number of offers from pro scouts, but his father's insistence that he attend college delayed those plans. After an outstanding athletic career at C.W. Post College on Long Island, Scheinblum and his father traveled to meet with two interested teams, the Pittsburgh Pirates and Cleveland Indians. The Indians offer of $12,000 per season, which was $4,000 more than the Pirates offered. This helped them to make their decision. Once he signed, Cleveland assigned him to their Class-A team in Burlington, North Carolina. He reached the majors in 1965, remaining in the Indians organization through the 1969 season until he was sold to the Washington Senators. In 1970, playing with the Senators' Minor League team in Wichita, Kansas, Scheinblum led that Double-A league with 79 runs, 265 total bases, 84 RBI's and tied with 155 hits. Those numbers earned him a promotion to Denver, Colorado. After hitting .388 in Denver in 1971, he was purchased by the Kansas City Royals. He enjoyed his best season in 1972 with the Royals, when he hit .300 as their everyday right fielder. He was named to the 1972 All-Star team and played in the game in Atlanta. He later played for the Cincinnati Reds, California Angels, and St. Louis Cardinals. He was also one of the first Jewish players to play professionally in Japan, where in 1975 and 1976 he played with the Hiroshima Toyo Carp. He retired in 1976 after having played in 462 games. A switch-hitter, his career average was .263 with 13 home runs and 127 RBI's. He was inducted into the C.W. Post University Athletic Hall of Fame in 2005. He lives in Palm Harbor, Florida.*

Tell me about your early years, growing up in the Bronx, and how you put yourself on the path to reach professional baseball.

RS: Well, I was born in 1942 in the Hell's Kitchen part of Manhattan and I grew up in the South Bronx. I used one address, but I had been in six different foster homes between the ages of two and seven. My brother Bob, I think, was in five different ones, and in two of them we stayed there together. My mom was ill in the hospital. My father took on a job and went to college at night, and every Sunday we got together and went to the hospital. Who knew things were bad until you look back on it? When I turned eight my mom died, and a while later my dad remarried and we moved to New Jersey. I actually started playing Little League when I was eight years old and at that time they only had one league for eight to twelve year olds. My brother was on a team, and he was eleven so they let me play also and as it turned out I was the starting left fielder. I was a tiny kid. When I turned twelve, I was the smallest kid in the entire league, four feet six inches tall. Even the eight year olds were bigger than me. As you play with better talent or bigger people you always get better. So I can attribute my brother getting me on the team to maybe the beginning of my success and getting to the big leagues.

You obviously overcame some hurdles at a young age with regard to your family situation. As you mentioned, your mother passed away when you were eight. Tell me about your father. He must have gone through a lot as well with her death and the thought of you and your brother being in foster homes. That had to be tough on him.

RS: He was a good man. It took him several years going to night school to get his CPA degree, so he worked during the day and went to school at night. After the new marriage, with the five of us all together, he put all of us through college. Well, in my case I was given one semester to get a scholarship, so I got the scholarship and my brother got it also. We each got a partial scholastic and the rest of it athletic, both of us. My brother went to a different college in New York though. I went to C.W. Post.

Some people faced with the circumstances you faced might find themselves headed down a troublesome road. You managed to keep things in a positive light and move forward in your life. How did you manage to remain positive? Did athletics and baseball play a part in that for you?

RS: Of course, it gave me something to do during the day. I enjoyed all the sports. I played basketball, I ran track, and I played baseball so each different season I had something to do. We were not allowed back in the house until the 6:00 p.m. dinner time so we were out playing, wherever it was unless it rained and we were then allowed back in the house. I think one of the problems with today's kids, and it is maybe not even their fault, but more time is spent playing baseball, basketball, and football video games than actually going out in the street and playing them. Even though today's athletes are bigger and stronger and probably much better, a lot of these players don't have the same history we had growing up. Also, the players during my time were all inner-city kids. The kids that went on to be doctors and lawyers and attorneys, they didn't have the same dream, maybe they did when they were younger, and I just kept the dream and I tried to pursue it.

Were any of these inner-city kids Jewish?

RS: Almost none.

With some of the other Jewish ballplayers I've talked with, their upbringing and family life were such that a major importance and emphasis in the home was placed on education more so than athletics. A career as a professional athlete was not something that was given serious consideration.

RS: Jewish kids don't play in the dirt.

Exactly. So, did you ever face any opposition from your father with regards to ever playing professionally?

RS: No, I had a nice backing from friends and close family, most of them anyway.

So there was never that feeling that, because I'm Jewish and because of that pervasive attitude that "Jews don't strive to become professional athletes," it was something you ever contemplated not doing?

RS: Oh, I was a different person for different occasions. When I played baseball, I was a baseball player; or when it came to religion, I was Jewish. Two separate things.

You received some offers and were obviously pretty good during your high school years. What kind of offers did you receive and from what teams?

RS: I was offered a couple of contracts, that to me were enormous amounts of money, $2,500, but my dad wouldn't let me take them. He wanted me to go to college. And as it worked out it was to my benefit and to my detriment. Coming out of college at twenty-one, all of a sudden I had lost four years to players that had signed at seventeen. They were much more seasoned and I had a lot of catching up to do.

Once again though, your father, in the end, knew how important an education would be to you later on in life.

RS: At one time I guess, he played tennis, but knew very little about baseball or any of the other sports. You know, he was good when we were outdoors playing them, just a nice man and he knew how important education was.

You ended up going to college and you attend C.W. Post University on Long Island. Tell me about that experience.

RS: They were just great years. I can't tell you how much I enjoyed C.W. Post. I still stay in touch with a bunch of old friends and they wouldn't care if I were an astronaut or a baseball player. We still treat each other the same. It's funny in a way because I would make fun of what they do and they made fun of what I did.

After you graduated, you and your father traveled to meet with a couple of teams, the Pittsburgh Pirates and Cleveland Indians.

RS: It was Pittsburgh first and my college baseball coach came with us. His name was Dom Anile. There was no draft, so I was invited to different parks around the country to try out so he came with my dad and me. We went to Pittsburgh and old Forbes Field, and I had a good workout there. They offered me more money than I had ever heard of in my life and I was ready to grab a pen, but my coach said, "No, we're going to other places first." My father and I almost passed out. We went to Cleveland and, stories have been written about the occasion, but I actually did jump across the desk, grabbed his pen and signed it before my coach could say anything.

You got assigned to their Minor League team in Burlington, North Carolina. What's it like for a young Jewish kid from New York to all of a sudden find himself in the South, in a small town like Burlington?

RS: I didn't know I was Jewish until I played there. As soon as they found out, they let me know every day. But I got along very well with them. It was just a different time.

It sounds like you made a fairly smooth adjustment from New York to being down South and playing in North Carolina?

RS: It made no difference to me; every place I went I enjoyed. If I lived in an apartment or on a park bench, that was home. So when I went to Burlington that was home for that period of time. I met a bunch of great players, nice people. Some of them are still friends of mine today.

How would you describe the South during the mid to late 1960's when you were playing there?

RS: It was a little different, of course, than New York or New Jersey. In Burlington, if I remember, there was one restaurant, the Southern Grill, and we ate there every day. Five of us lived in the upstairs of a house. We kind of all drank a lot in those days before we found out that it hurt. It hurt your performance, but it was just fun. I enjoyed playing and it was just a good experience and good character building.

Where did you go after Burlington?

RS: Well, I hit .309 there, and that was in Class-B ball. I actually got sent to Class-C ball out to the California League and that year was the first year of the expansion. I was one of the protected players by Cleveland, one of the fifteen. I spent the first month up in Cleveland where he got one at-bat in four games scoring one run. Then they sent me to the California League in Salinas, California and then I came back up at the end of the year in 1965.

How exciting was that?

RS: Oh, very exciting! I had never even met a Major League Baseball player. Actually the first Major League game that I ever went to was the first one I played in.

Did it ever cross your mind that there were not a lot of Jews playing Major League ball or was that not a factor to you?

RS: It was brought up to me later on, but it was something that I just didn't even notice. They were just other players and then I found out, at the time, that there were just four or five of us of us in the big leagues. There was Ken Holtzman and Mike Epstein, Larry Sherry was still playing, and there was Steve Stone and Ronnie Blomberg. I think Ronnie came two or three years after. So there were a handful of us.

Do you remember if you ever faced any of the Jewish pitchers when you were playing?

RS: No. I've actually never even met Steve Stone. He was mostly in the National League and I was in the American League. We did not cross paths in the minor leagues. I'd actually like to face him, to see what he throws. Well, maybe not right now!

You spent time with the Washington Senators in 1971, played in 27 games, 49 at-bats and then finished the year in Double-A in Denver. You hit .388 in 106 games with 145 hits, 31 doubles and 25 home runs. In 1972 you were in Kansas City playing for the Royals and had a great season, making the American League All-Star team.

RS: Yes, I did. It was a great thrill. I was leading the major leagues in hitting at the All-Star break. Throughout my career I could never hit in April. For some reason my fingers swelled. I don't think I ever hit over .200 in any April of any season. I mentioned it to the coaches and they really didn't want to hear about it, so a lot of times I'd make the team out of spring training and they'd bring me up, and I would do absolutely nothing and they'd send me back down. Even growing up in New York, I never ice skated or anything. I just did not like the cold weather that much.

What do you remember about being in Atlanta and playing in the All-Star game?

RS: I remember two great thrills from that game. One is that I was one of the four players from the American League that was used for the press conference and there were four from the National League. I was going to be the first speaker and at the time I was the headliner. I was leading both leagues in hitting, and I was getting ready to stand up and someone tapped me on the shoulder and said, "Richie, I have an important engagement. Will you mind if I go on up before you?" It was Willie Mays. Growing up, he and Mickey Mantle were my two favorite players and I'd never met Willie before. I'd played against him, and I said, "Of course." The other great thing was, I think in the sixth or seventh inning, Hank Aaron hit the home run and he was already into his forties and the ground shook. It was very exciting. Just a nice occasion.

You spent some time as well in Cincinnati with the Reds and then in California with the Angels.

RS: I think that the Angels were probably my favorite team because of Gene Autry. He was a nice man.

I also read that for a while, you roomed with teammate and fellow Jewish player Mike Epstein.

RS: Yes, and I also roomed with Steve Barber after Mike left, and Steve recently passed away. Mike and I roomed together in Washington and then with the Angels. I'll tell you, his shoulders could fill up a room. Mike's a large man.

Did you consider yourself a religious person during your baseball career?

RS: Well, I'm not Hassidic, but I'm a nice Jew.

Like Greenberg and Koufax during their careers, did you ever face a situation where you had to make a decision not to play because of a Jewish holiday?

RS: I did while I was playing in Japan. Hiroshima, the team I played for, in the thirty years they had the league, they'd come in last place twenty-nine times and fifth place once. So the first year I went there we won the pennant, and we went into the Japanese World Series. When Yom Kippur came, I tried to explain, being the first Jew that had ever played there, that I couldn't play, that it was my day of one on one with God, but they didn't quite understand. So I didn't play, and I heard a knock on my door while I was at home, and here comes something like a hundred reporters. They wanted to watch me pray. Very funny! That is the one time where I respected my religion with baseball.

How did you find the experience of playing baseball in Japan? You were there for what, a couple of years?

RS: I was there for two years. Day to day at times it was a problem, but looking back it was just an incredible cultural experience.

At that time too you did not have the best Japanese players coming to the United States to play here like many do today. The best players stayed there and played.

RS: They had a bunch of players that easily could have played here. Sadahara Oh was a good solid hitter. They had some decent pitching, and fundamentally they were good players, except they were all set into one mold. Only the great players jumped out of the mold and used their own creative abilities.

After playing in Japan for those two seasons, when did you know that it was time to give up baseball?

RS: It was actually by mistake. I was with St. Louis, and they told me I'd been traded to the Dodgers. I had some friends on the Dodgers but growing up in New York, it just came into my head. I'm from the Bronx and I was a big Giants fan, and a Giants fan does not want to play with the Dodgers. So I was offered a nice amount of money to play in Japan. I asked St. Louis if they would release me, and they did, so I went to Japan instead of going to the Dodgers. Looking back I probably should have gone. But already arthritis had set in, and I was beginning to feel pain in my joints. It probably was a good move going over. It's hard to second guess yourself. Who knows if it was good or bad?

What was life like for your when your baseball career came to an end?

RS: Well, I had a business background, and my wife had a college degree. I asked her about opening up a store; what would you like to sell? She said "I like jewelry," so she ran the front and I ran the back, the business end while she did the buying and selling, and it worked out very well.

So today you are retired?

RS: I sell promotional products. They're items with logos on it. I try to be sophisticated by saying promotional products.

Is there overall satisfaction when you look back on your baseball career?

RS: Ah, yes and no. Every time I struck out maybe I would like to go back and see that same pitch again. There is no way you can second guess or change anything. You did it, and I enjoyed every minute of it. I had some good years and some bad years, but overall I think I was a good solid average Major League Baseball player. Not the best, not the worst.

*"My first time at bat we were playing against Cleveland,
and I was batting against Bob Lemon, a Hall of Fame pitcher.
He got me to 3-2, and I hadn't swung the bat.
The next pitch he threw in the dirt, and I walked.
I'll tell you what, my knees were shaking. I will never forget that."*

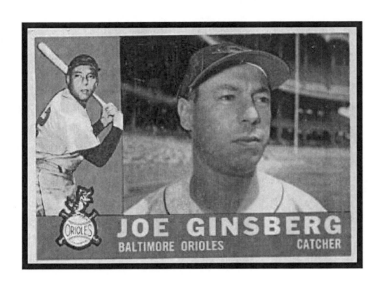

JOE GINSBERG

Born in New York in 1926 and adopted by the Ginsberg family a couple of months later, young Myron never knew his biological parents. He took to the nickname "Little Joe" from an early age after his adoptive father, and the name stuck with him throughout his life and career. He grew up in Detroit when Hank Greenberg was one of the stars of baseball, but he never had an interest in going to watch the Tigers play. A very good athlete in high school, especially excelling at baseball, **Joe Ginsberg** *was drafted by the Tigers in 1944 at the age of 17. Little did he know at that time that he would enjoy a well-traveled thirteen-year career, spending time with the Detroit Tigers, Cleveland Indians, Kansas City Athletics, Baltimore Orioles, Chicago White Sox, Boston Red Sox, and New York Mets. Highlights throughout his career include catching Virgil Truck's two no-hitters in 1952, helping the Indians to the 1954 American League Pennant, being with the Red Sox on the day that Roger Maris hit his 61st home run in 1961, and he was one of the original Mets, being behind the plate for the team's first ever game in New York. In 695 games, his career batting average was .241 with 20 home runs and 182 RBI's. He played his final game on April 15, 1962. He now lives in Lake Suze, Florida.*

Joe, tell me a little about your early years and how your love for baseball developed.

JG: Well, I was born in New York, but I was adopted by these two Jewish people who got me right out of the hospital when I was like two months old. These two people took me in and raised me, and I couldn't have had a better mother and father than my adopted parents.

Do you know whether or not your biological parents were in fact Jewish?

JG: I have no idea. I couldn't tell you that. I was just a baby and they adopted me, and I never did know who my real parents were. I'm sorry to say, but that's the way it was. I've had a great life with these two Jewish people, and they treated me just great all throughout grade school and high school and everything like that, and they supported me throughout my baseball career too.

Did you grow up in an observant Jewish household?

JG: Well, yes, I had my bar mitzvah and everything like that, but I never really went to the shul or temple. I was never really religious, I'm sorry to say, because I was always playing sports, and I just didn't have time to do anything like that. Actually, I probably missed a lot by not doing that, but with baseball and basketball in high school, I was a pretty good athlete and that was it.

The fact that you were a good athlete in high school, was that kind of the basis for your popularity in the neighborhood?

JG: Yes, I think so. Once you start playing sports and you're on the high school baseball team and basketball team, you are sort of respected by a lot of the students then.

You grew up in Detroit when Hank Greenberg was a star for the Tigers. Was he someone that you followed and looked up to?

JG: Well, he wasn't my idol; he was my father's idol. I would rather play baseball than watch it. I never did go down to see Hank play because I always wanted to play myself, but I did get to know Hank Greenberg when he was the General Manager of the Cleveland Indians. I got traded to Cleveland and that is when I got to know Hank pretty good. The only trouble was that they had a catcher named Jim Hegan who did a lot of catching, and that's when I had to ask Hank, "What in the world did you trade for me for because you've got Jim Hegan over there who's doing all the catching and I'm just sitting there watching him?" I didn't want that. I wanted to go out and play and he said, "Well Joe, I'll give you a chance and see if I can't make a trade for you." They did, so I got to Baltimore, where I got to play a lot. Gus Triandos was the other catcher, and Gus hit against the left-handed pitchers. I hit against the right-handed pitchers being a left-handed hitter. So that was just fine, but I did not want to just go around and sit and watch somebody else play.

So then, how old were you when Greenberg was playing in Detroit?

JG: Oh, I was going to high school then. I was fifteen, sixteen, seventeen years old. I never did go down to Tiger Stadium. Only once when we played down there they invited a lot of us that played American Legion ball down to, it was Briggs Stadium then, and we had a game and that was the first time I ever saw Briggs Stadium.

Did it ever really dawn on you that Hank Greenberg was Jewish? I know that with some of the other Jewish players, depending upon what city they played in, it seemed like the Jewish community there would kind of adopt them as "their own" player.

JG: Well, that never happened to me for some reason because, being that we weren't in a Jewish neighborhood, I was probably one of the only Jewish fellas in the school, and in the neighborhood there weren't any Jewish people. Why my dad and mother moved to a place like that I'll never know, but I made some great friends and even today I communicate with some of the people I used to know.

But when you were in Detroit during those years, was Greenberg the kind of player that the Jewish community in Detroit gravitated to?

JG: Oh, without a doubt because he hit 58 home runs one year and he was a home run hitter, a big strong guy and he did a lot for the Detroit Tigers. As a matter of fact, I think they were in the World Series with Hank one year. He just was one of the big stars for the Detroit Tigers for a long time.

As it turned out, coming out of high school, you get drafted by the Tigers. That must have been exciting to have been drafted by your hometown team.

JG: Well, that's true. One of the scouts, Wes Hugan, signed all the Detroit guys like Hal Newhouser, Johnny Lipon, Ted Gray, and Billy Pierce. We were all Detroit boys who had all played against one another in the sandlot, and I'll be darned if we weren't all on the Tigers together. That was really nice.

By that time, was Greenberg still on the scene or was he not in Detroit at all anymore?

JG: Oh, he was gone by then. Hank was a lot older than me anyway, you know, so I never did know Greenberg as a one-on-one. It was as a general manager and a player. That's the only way I knew him.

How did the negotiations go once the Tigers drafted you? Did Detroit's Jewish community ever take notice?

JG: No, I'll be darned. I never did read anything about it or things like that. I was seventeen years old, and I was going into the twelfth grade. All of a sudden when these scouts came over to my house to try and sign me, they came over to the house, and my dad was there, and they said that they wanted me to sign a contract with a Class-D team in the minor leagues in Jamestown, New York. I told my dad that I wanted to quit school, and I wanted to go and play professional ball. He said, "Well, why don't you find out what kind of money they are going to pay you before you do that?" and I said, "Well dad, I don't know. I guess I should do that," so I did. I asked the scout, "Well, how much money will I get?" And they said, "We give all guys that start out in Class-D a hundred dollars a month." My dad said, "How in the world do you expect them to get by on a hundred dollars a month?" I told my dad that I would get by one way or another, but I was wrong. I had to come and tell my dad that I needed a little money at the end of the month, you know, and he would send ten bucks or something like that, so I got by alright. Then, when I turned eighteen, well the next thing you know I got drafted into the Army. I went to Fort Ord in Northern California for basic training. After that I was on a ship going to Manila while the war was still going on. When I was in the war there, in the Philippines, I was walking around the compound one day and I heard the crack of a bat, and I said, "Oh my God, there's a baseball game going on somewhere around the fields there!" I walked around and sure enough there was a baseball game going on. I saw one of the lieutenants there. He was one of the guys trying to get the teams together, and I said, "Lieutenant, what's going on here?" He answered, "Well, we're going to get a baseball team." And he said, "Why? Did you ever play in high school? I said, "Oh jeez, I had one year of pro." Well, when he found out that I had one year of pro he just said, "Get him a uniform. We want him to play with us." Well, that kept me from going into combat, so I was very fortunate there. They finally sent me to Manila to play in what they called the big leagues with guys like Early Wynn, Max Macon, and Joe Garagiola. We had a big league team, and that's what I did for about eighteen months: play baseball and entertain the troops. So I was very fortunate to not have to go into combat.

So, in a way, baseball may have saved your life.

JG: I agree. I say that because some of the young fellas that were eighteen, nineteen years old, we were what they called "replacements" for the guys that were getting shot, getting wounded, and getting killed. Then they'd put a truckload of guys on the truck, send them up to the mountains, and they were replacements. That's what I was going to do if it wasn't for baseball, and who knows what would have happened.

You mentioned signing with the Tigers and the discussion that went on with your father just prior to that. In some of my other interviews with Jewish players, some of them had parents that frowned on bypassing an education for a professional baseball career. At that time they just did not perceive that playing baseball was a way to make a living. Did your parents have a similar attitude? Did they want you to go to college instead?

JG: Well, I don't know if my father ever thought I would ever make a living at it, but even when we were just little guys playing American Legion ball, my dad would have a car and he would drive a lot of us to the ball game. Maybe four or five players would fit in my dad's car, and he would drive us out to the ball field and wait for us, put us back in the car, and drive us back into the neighborhood. He really supported me, but he let me do just about what I wanted to do. And what I wanted to do was play baseball. That's really what I wanted to do, and I never thought I would make a career out of it, but gee whiz, I played in the minor leagues for five years, and the big leagues for thirteen years, and two years in the Army, so that's about twenty years of professional baseball.

In 1944, at the age of seventeen, you embark on your pro career, starting out in the minor leagues in Jamestown, New York. What was that like?

JG: It was a beautiful little town. Our center fielder was Nellie Fox, the future great second baseman for the Chicago White Sox. He played center field for the Jamestown Falcons. I was there and I was a catcher, so that's when I knew Nellie Fox. Then I got to know Nellie real well after I got traded to the White Sox also.

So, you were drafted into the service in 1944-45. When you returned in 1947, you were twenty years old, and you were first assigned to Williamsport, Pennsylvania.

JG: That was a Detroit Tigers farm team, and I had a real good year down there. I wound up leading the league in hitting. I hit .326, and right then the Tigers brought me up.

What were you thinking at that point? Here you are. You're twenty years old and the Tigers call you up from Single-A ball to the major leagues?

JG: Oh, my God! I mean, I was scared to death. Williamsport was Class-A and in those years there was Class A, B, C, AA, AAA, etc. and then the big leagues. Well, I got called right up from the Class-A, and here I am in the big leagues with a Detroit uniform on, and I said, "Oh my God!" Playing in my hometown, and doing everything like this. There are very few baseball players that play four or five years on their own hometown, and I was very fortunate to do that.

Do you remember your first time you stepped to the plate to hit?

JG: Oh, yeah. My first time at bat we were playing against Cleveland, and I was batting against Bob Lemon, a Hall of Fame pitcher, and I never got to swing the bat. He got me to 3-2, and I hadn't swung the bat. The next pitch he threw in the dirt, and I walked. I'll tell you what, my knees were shaking. I will never forget that.

Did you keep the bat and ball from that first at-bat?

JG: No I didn't. I never was one to be keeping things like that. I probably should have, but I never did.

In 1949 you were back in the minors, playing in Toledo, and you had a great year there. Then you were right back up in the majors with the Tigers.

JG: That's right. I had my mind made up that I wasn't going to be a Minor League baseball player. I was going to be a big leaguer. I wound up having thirteen years in the big leagues and I'm very proud of that.

In 1951, you finally broke through and became the Tigers' starting catcher.

JG: Red Rolfe liked the way I played. He liked the way I swung the bat, and I wound up catching just about every day and had a pretty good year. The knock on me was that I did not hit enough home runs. I hit about eight or ten home runs, and when I went up to sign my contract, that's what they said. They said, "Jeez Joe, you only hit like ten home runs, and we want a catcher that can hit between twenty and twenty-five." Well I just said, "Why didn't you tell me that? I didn't know that. I mean if you had told me you wanted twenty to twenty-five, I'd have tried." I didn't know what to say to them. I didn't like that they'd put a knock on me that I didn't hit enough home runs. I never was a home run hitter, but I would have tried to hit a few more if I'd known that's what they wanted.

When you were in the minor leagues, did you ever face any prejudices or deal with verbal abuse from opposing players or fans because you were Jewish?

JG: You can't miss it. You hear it once in a while coming out of the stands. Even the ballplayers once in a while will say something about Jews and this and that, but you just got to let the water run off your back. You can't be the kind of guy who wants to fight all the time if they say something about your religion. Even though I was never really religious, with my name, it was synonymous with Jewish people, so you're bound to hear it. There's always anti-Semitism around, and you're going to hear it. Just like black guys heard it with them, the Jewish boys heard it, too.

In 1953 you were traded to the Cleveland Indians. How did you feel about that at the time?

JG: Yes, I got traded to Cleveland, and that's when Hank Greenberg was the General Manager. About a month into the season I didn't want to stay there because I wasn't playing. I told Mr. Greenberg, "I don't know why you got me over here because I want to play. I don't want to sit there and watch somebody else play." So, sure enough I got traded and that's what I wanted. I wanted to get out of there. I wanted to play, not sit there and watch somebody else play and, that's the way I've been. I've lived my life like that. I've just wanted to play all the time.

Following your stint in Cleveland, you spent time in Indianapolis, Seattle, Kansas City, Baltimore, Chicago, Boston, Denver, and New York. Didn't that get tiring after a while going from team to team?

JG: No. It's not tiring if you stay in the big leagues. That's the answer. A lot of people said, "Well Joe, didn't anybody want you? You got traded seven times." I said, "Are you kidding? Everybody wanted me. When you play for seven teams, you know you are in demand." That's the way I looked at it anyway, and it worked out okay for me.

After spending time in the minor leagues with Indianapolis and then Seattle, you made it back to the majors with Kansas City in 1956.

JG: That's right. Lou Boudreau was the manager. He said they were going to play me, but sure enough I played in sixty or seventy games. I had a pretty good year. I didn't have a bad year there. We didn't have a very good year that year with the Kansas City Athletics. They were not in the league that long, I don't know, they were the Philadelphia Athletics and then the Kansas City Athletics, and then I don't know where they went.

You were present for some historic events, one of them being the game in which Roger Maris hit his 61st home run. It was 1961, and you were with the Red Sox.

JG: I guess so. I didn't know that. I know that Roger hit 61 and Mantle hit 56 or something like that. Those guys were some one-two punch for the Yankees that year, I'll tell ya.

You closed out your career in 1962 with the New York Mets.

JG: Yeah, I caught the first game that the Mets ever played in New York. I was about at the end of my career in 1962, and I got released. All of a sudden I get a call from the Mets, and they said "We're going to get a team here in New York called the New York Mets, and we're looking for players. How would you like to come over and play for the New York Mets?" I said, "Well, I've just been released and I'm thirty-six years old, but I'd be glad to come." So I did, and, I'll be darned, Old Casey Stengel called me into the office and he said, "You are going to catch opening day with the New York Mets." I said, "Isn't that something?" That was the first game the Mets ever played in New York. I really enjoyed that, and now they call us the Original Mets. That was Ritchie Ashburn, Gil Hodges and there are a lot of them that are not around anymore. Casey knew that though. He said, "You'll get more recognition catching the first game that the Mets ever played than you did in your whole thirteen year career." I thought he was just talking, but I'll be darned if he wasn't right about that.

After thirteen years of professional baseball, how did you know that it was time to consider retirement?

JG: Well, you know, baseball players, once you're at the end of your career, no one has to tell you. You know that your skills are gone, your legs aren't there anymore, you're not swinging the bat good, and you don't have to have anybody tell you. You know that you're not going to play. When I got released from the Mets, I came back to Detroit, and I'll be darned if I don't get a call from Jim Campbell, who was the General Manager of the Detroit Tigers, and I said, "Ah Jim, don't tell me you want me to come play for you now," and he said, "No Joe, I'll tell you what I'd like to have you do. We just signed a kid out of the University of Michigan, and he's a catcher. We sent him down to Denver and I'd like to have you go down to Denver and try to work with him a little bit and answer his questions." I said, "I'd be glad to do that after we talk money." When we got that straightened out, I went down there, and who do you think the guy is down there? It's Bill Freehan. So Bill Freehan calls me the "mentor" now because I did show him a few things that I thought would improve his catching ability. Bill was just a big, strong guy and he had a pretty darned good career with the Detroit Tigers.

Was managing or coaching something you thought you might be interested in once your playing career came to an end?

JG: Yes, I thought I'd like that. Being a catcher, you know catchers make good managers and coaches. But I did like to play and I knew my skills were gone, so I just came home and got myself an honest job. I went to work with the Jack Daniels distillery and represented them for sixteen years. I really had a good job. I had the state of Michigan for them.

Was it tough to get baseball and the baseball lifestyle out of your system?

JG: Well, it just never got out of my system because they always call you back to Old-Timers' Day. Then I worked the fantasy camps for the Tigers for a while. As a matter of fact, for six or seven years, Virgil Trucks and Mickey Lolich and I worked the fantasy camps, which was a lot of fun. It was good money; they paid us pretty good. There were doctors and lawyers and well-to-do businessman who were living out their fantasy. They wanted to be baseball players, and we gave them their own uniforms with their name on the back. It was just a ball. I had so much fun during those six or seven years. It was really good.

It sounds to me like you consider yourself, out of all the teams you played for, a Detroit Tiger at heart?

JG: No doubt about it. Detroit's my home town, and I played for them and wanted to play for them. Most guys that grew up in Detroit wanted to play for the Detroit Tigers, there's no doubt about it. Not very many of us get to do that.

Are you just living the retired life now?

JG: Oh yes. I'm retired and I live in Florida. A place called Lake Suze, on the fifteenth green of my country club, which is the King's Lake Country Club. I play golf about four times a week, and just enjoy my life as much as I can without my wife. She passed away on May 24, 2006. It's a different lifestyle, but I'm getting by okay.

"I got called up on a Monday. I got called into manager Larry Doby's office. He said, 'You're starting Wednesday.' So, I went out and threw on the side, shagged some balls in the outfield. I think the first thing I did when I found out was I called my parents and my brother and sister. I was very excited."

ROSS BAUMGARTEN

Ross Baumgarten *was born in 1955 in Highland Park, Illinois and grew up a Chicago Cubs fan in Glencoe, Illinois. A very good athlete who had an interest in a variety of sports, Baumgarten eventually found that baseball was his passion. As he progressed through New Trier High School, he seemed to come into his own during his senior season, enough to attract the attention of the college scouts. He began his collegiate career at Florida Southern University before the lack of playing time there encouraged him to transfer to Palm Beach Community College. From there he signed on to play at the University of Florida where he would become a member of what were some very competitive Gator teams. He was selected by the Chicago White Sox in the twentieth round of the 1977 Major League Baseball amateur draft. In 1978 he accomplished a rare feat, posting a winning record at every level in professional baseball. He started the season at Single-A Appleton, Wisconsin where he went 9-1, followed by a 2-1 stint with Double-A Knoxville, Tennessee. He was 5-4 while pitching at Triple-A Des Moines, Iowa and then finally 2-2 when called up to finish out the season in Chicago with the White Sox. His best season came in 1979, going 13-8 with an ERA of 3.53 (9th in the American League). He was named Co-Rookie of the Year by the Chicago Baseball Writers. Following a trade to the Pittsburgh Pirates in March of 1982, he played in twelve games with the Pirates before being released in March of 1983. His overall career record was 22-36 with an ERA of 4.02. He played in 90 games, making 84 starts. His last game was on August 23, 1982. He lives in his hometown of Glencoe.*

Tell me a little about your early years and your interest in sports and baseball in particular.

RB: I grew up in Northern Illinois in a town called Glencoe, and I was interested in all the sports. But my favorite was always baseball. I grew up playing it day and night, summer, spring, and fall, but obviously couldn't do much in the winter. It was always my first love, and I was always going to try and keep playing until they told me I couldn't.

How were your parents concerning your interest in athletics? Were they supportive, or were they more interested in making sure that you took care of your academics?

RB: Well, my parents, self-admittedly, were not really involved in my baseball playing to the point of pushing me. They would come to the games. Back in those days you weren't going to get lessons all the time from people, so you just were going out a lot and playing on playgrounds, inventing games or playing pick-up games with your friends. You know, it was all very kid-centric back in those days, and we were just having fun. I just picked up enough skills through the days and got good enough that I got the opportunity to play Major League Baseball.

The reason that I asked that question goes back to the pervasive attitude in many Jewish households, that the parents, for the most part, really push academics. Sports are not viewed as something that can become a "career." That's why there is the on-going stereotype that there are so many Jewish professionals such as doctors, dentists, and lawyers, etc. Did you grow up in that kind of a home?

RB: Yeah, you know, it was not a very religious household. My parents were divorced when I was eight and there was never any steering away from athletics. Back in those days it was just innocent fun. It was not as high pressured and high powered as it is now. I'm sure that they didn't give any thought to me making it professionally, but it was always a goal of mine. From the very first that I can remember, I wanted to play in the major leagues. I grew up a big Chicago Cubs fan and would watch all the games on TV that I could. In those days you basically had your local game and you had the game of the week. Now you can watch three or four games every night if you want. But, I was just going to keep going. I mean, it was my goal. I'm sure they probably thought that at some point I'd stop and I would go on to more of a doctor, lawyer or whatever type career. You know, it didn't quite happen that way. I actually made it, so it worked out for me.

It seems like you really began to find your groove in baseball as a senior in high school.

RB: Well, in grade school I was always the best player on the team. I got into high school, in a big high school that was very competitive, and I grew much later than everyone else so, while I had what I thought was equal ability, I was much smaller than everyone else. I couldn't throw the ball as hard. But when I finally grew my junior year, basically grew a foot in height and added fifty pounds in weight, I got on a level playing field with the other kids. Then I was back to being pretty good again, so I had a nice senior year in high school. That led me to some colleges that were pretty high powered. I always worked hard, tried to keep improving, and listened and watched what the pros were doing because I had to rely on being smarter than most. I wasn't gifted with a ninety mile an hour fastball or anything like that, so I had to be smarter than the average guy. I worked hard at it and it worked out.

So you started your college baseball career at Florida Southern College. What was that like for you, going from high school ball to college ball?

RB: I went to Florida Southern College, which was one of the top Division II schools at the time, and I believe that they still are. A high school teammate of mine went to Rollins College, which was a similar school in Orlando. Florida Southern was in Lakeland, and, you know, I just walked-on. I actually had a really good fall season there, but the politics of the baseball team were that most of the kids were junior college transfers with scholarships, so the coaching staff had money invested in them, and they didn't have anything invested in me. While I felt I was just as good as they were, and my statistics in the fall showed that, I was kind of left by the wayside in the spring as a member of the junior varsity or freshman team, whatever it was called at the time. And when it came time to decide what I was going to do, I wasn't going to do that my sophomore year because I wanted to play. Those guys would then be back as seniors, so I decided to transfer to a junior college, which was the only way you could actually be eligible and pitch the next year. You couldn't go from a four-year school to a four-year school, so I went to Palm Beach Junior College.

And from there you end up going to the University of Florida?

RB: It was a good move as it turned out. Palm Beach needed pitchers; they were an up and coming program. I ended up the number one pitcher, had a very significant sophomore season, and ended up with ten, fifteen scholarship offers to go back to a four-year school. I ended up at the University of Florida from there.

Did you have any opportunities to sign coming out of high school?

RB: No opportunities out of high school. None after my year in Palm Beach, when a lot of junior college kids get drafted. I wasn't a finished product yet. I got a late start because I didn't pitch as a sophomore or junior in high school, and I didn't really get to pitch a lot as a freshman in college. So I'd kind of gone pretty far for a guy who hadn't pitched much, but I still had so much to learn and improve upon. And then my junior year at Florida I was ineligible due to a transfer violation. The NCAA, in all of its wisdom, decided that I had taken a course at the University of Florida when I should have taken a course at Palm Beach Junior College. You know, in my opinion, where would you rather have a kid take the course, at the four-year school or the two-year school? They decided that I should be ineligible for that "massive" violation. I showed up in court in Tallahassee, and I had one twenty-three-year-old lawyer right out of law school and the NCAA, the SEC, the University of Florida, I don't know, there must have been eight lawyers there against me because I felt like maybe I'd committed murder in the first degree the way there was eight lawyers there against me. You know, ultimately, the judge ruled against me so I had to sit out my junior year. Now, if you look at my seven years of high school and college, I'd only pitched in two of the seven really. I was invited to play baseball in the Cape Cod summer league. It is where a lot of the top college pitchers go, so I was able to have a nice summer season there and get back into the shape of things. That led to my senior year at Florida, senior year in school but actually only a junior year in eligibility. I had a nice year. We were ranked fourth in the country at one point, finished eleventh, missed out on going to the college world series by one game. You know, I had a nice year and then got drafted by the White Sox.

You got drafted by the White Sox in the twentieth round of the 1977 Major League Baseball amateur draft. You mentioned earlier that you had grown up a Cubs fan. Still, how exciting was it for you to be drafted by one of your home town teams?

RB: The University of Florida sports information director called me the morning after the draft. In those days you didn't really know what was going on; it wasn't like ESPN was around. So, he said, "I've got good news and bad news," and I said, "What's the good news?" He said "You got drafted." I had gone to bed that night thinking I wasn't drafted and, you know, thinking that maybe my career would be over. I said "That's great. What could possibly be the bad news?" He said, "You got drafted by the White Sox," because he knew I was a Cubs fan. I quickly became a Sox fan and progressed through the system.

Were there any memorable experiences from your stay in the minor leagues? It looks like you were not in the minors for very long.

RB: The minors is an interesting thing. You're thrown together with a lot of people from a lot of different places. A lot of kids that hadn't gone to college. I had been to college. There were others that had been to college, there were some kids from Mexico, you know, just thrown together in a whole potpourri of people. I got sent to Appleton, Wisconsin, which was Class-A ball. Just a horrible team. I think we lost a hundred games that year; I was only around for half of it. It went pretty well for me. I do remember one night we played a doubleheader and we lost both games as usual and the games ended at like 12:00, 12:30 a.m. and the manager says, "I'll see you here at six" and some guy said, "6:00 p.m.?" and he goes, "No, I want you here and dressed at 6:00 a.m." So there we were, congregated in the dugout at 6:00 a.m., not a lot of sleep, not too happy about it, certainly not anything we'd been through before, and he proceeded to talk for three hours about all of the things that we had been doing wrong. That has always stuck in my memory.

So you were only in the minors in 1978?

RB: Well, I finished 1977 in the minors, which would have been half of June, July, and August. I went back to school to do a little work. The 1978 season started. I was sent back to Appleton. By now we were a good team. I believe we were the only team in pro ball that year to win over a hundred games; we were something like 105-40. I mean, it was just an amazing season but I was only around until June. You know, we were a good team. We were scoring a lot of runs. We started out 9-1, fairly dominant. They then moved me to Knoxville, Tennessee, which was Double-A. I spent two weeks there. I made a couple of starts and one relief appearance, and I did fairly well. They moved me to Des Moines, Iowa, which was Triple-A. Spent the end of June to mid-August in Des Moines; I believe it was six weeks. I was doing well there. I had a winning record on a losing team. Then in mid-August they called me to the big leagues, so I did a lot of traveling that year, a lot of moving into apartments and a lot of moving out and turning on electricity and phones and turning them off, but it was fun. I got there in one year. I think at the time, it was only the second time in the history of baseball that a guy had gone through every level of the minors and then made the majors in one season. So, it was kind of fun.

Tell me about your first time taking the field as a Major Leaguer.

RB: Oh sure. I got called up on a Monday. I got called into manager Larry Doby's office. He said, "You're starting Wednesday." So, I went out and threw on the side, shagged some balls in the outfield. I think the first thing I did when I found out was I called my parents and my brother and sister. I was very excited. You know, Wednesday night we beat Texas. It was in Texas and we won, I'm not even sure of the score, but I pitched like six innings and gave up two runs, I believe, and did okay. I remember coming off the field in the sixth inning when I got replaced, and sitting right at the dugout were my brother and my father. My father had flown in from Chicago and my brother had flown in from Los Angeles and they didn't tell me, so it was kind of neat to see them there.

Two of your more memorable pitching performances were one-hitters that you threw in 1979 and 1980. What do you remember about those games?

RB: They were both against the California Angels. One of them, I think, I gave up a hit in the sixth inning to Bobby Grich. The second one I gave up a hit to Rod Carew in the seventh. I had him struck out, but the umpire wouldn't call the pitch. You know, Rod Carew got a little protection in those days. But I have it on tape, and if you saw the pitch, it was a strike. They were obviously very exciting. One of the games, the first one, I didn't finish. I think it was a combined one-hitter, and I walked a lot of guys if I remember. The second one was more of a classic game one-hitter. I don't believe I walked many guys, and you know, it was great fun. One thing I remember about the first one was, I believe it was the same day as there was a major plane crash at O'Hare in which a lot of people died, and the second one I remember because before the game one of the radio guys, Jimmy Piersall, had attacked one of the sports writers, and I was one of the guys to break it up. I guess I needed momentous events to throw well.

You had a pretty good season in 1979, making the Topps All-Star Rookie team.

RB: Yes, I was. I came in second in the rookie voting to one of my high school teammates and another guy. I had a nice year. You know, I was healthy; I was consistent. I was 13-8 with a good ERA on a team that lost 90 games or so. I had three of four games where I left late with leads that were eventually lost, so I could have won even more. Actually, the second year, I pitched better. I had some arm issues, but I had actually pitched better, and I just didn't get any support. In my twenty-four starts we scored twenty-five runs while I was in the game, so it's hard to win when you're getting one run a game. It was a lot of pressure on me, but it was just part of the experience.

By then you began to develop shoulder problems. Did your shoulder become even more of a problem?

RB: Yes, I had some shoulder issues on and off, but they really didn't become a major problem until 1982. I was one of those guys that was a little undersized and had to put more effort into each pitch; it didn't come as naturally and free-flowing. So I think the over-exertion finally caught up to me. In those days we had some workouts similar to what they do today, but we did not know nearly what they know today even though they get hurt today too. It's just an occupational hazard.

It sounds similar to what I always thought about a pitcher like Pedro Martinez, a guy who is smaller in physical stature but who throws the ball really hard. It looks strenuous when you watch him throw.

RB: Right. I had to use more energy and more effort every pitch, but obviously he's a lot better than I was and threw a lot more. But, you know, eventually most of us have some issues somewhere along the line.

When you were with the White Sox, you were on the team with both Ron Blomberg and Steve Stone. Is that correct?

RB: Yes, when I joined the Sox in 1978, Blomberg and Stoney were there.

Was anything ever made of that, the fact that there were three Jewish players on the club?

RB: No, not really, maybe among ourselves a little bit. You know, I don't think that anyone was walking around wearing a sign saying, "I'm Jewish." Teammates didn't care, but it was kind of like a thing between the three of us—how many teams have three? It wasn't anything that was played up within the team or in the press or anywhere, at least to my recollection.

Your career ended in Pittsburgh with the Pirates?

RB: Yes, I got traded at the beginning of 1982 to the Pirates.

Was that a little bit sad or discouraging to get traded away from your home city of Chicago, a town that you enjoyed playing in?

RB: You know, it was in the sense that Pittsburgh is not one of my favorite towns, and the city was not very supportive of the team, so I went from a very rambunctious atmosphere to the catacombs, but it's what happens. After I was there and during one of my first starts, I broke a knuckle. Then I came back and hurt my shoulder, and that was the end of it. I never really could throw well again.

Have you ever thought about the fact that you're part of a small percentage that ever makes the major leagues to begin with, and then within that group, you are part of an even smaller select group, being a Jewish ballplayer who makes it to the majors? Was it something you ever thought about?

RB: Not really. You know, other than this set of baseball cards that was put together four of five years ago, other than that nothing's ever really been done with it, so it's not like there have been a lot of great accolades about it. As I told you before, I don't really focus on religion. I was just a kid who loved to pitch, loved to learn about how to become a better pitcher, took the challenge of getting Major League hitters out very, very seriously, and that's really what my focus was.

Who were some of the toughest hitters you faced during your time in the major leagues?

RB: The toughest was Paul Molitor. He was just a good hitter. He could pull the ball, and he could hit it to right field. In those days all the power hitters were pull hitters. Here was a guy who could hit for power, didn't hit a lot of home runs but he hit the ball hard, you know, doubles, triples kind of thing and he would hit it everywhere, so he was always kind of difficult for me.

When did it dawn on you that it was time to retire from baseball, and do you remember what it was like to wake up the first "morning after" realizing that you're not playing Major League Baseball anymore?

RB: Well, I had known throughout the 1983 season when I had tried to come back in the minors that my arm just wasn't getting better, and I just wasn't able to get people out anymore. In those days you didn't have multi-year contracts, for the most part, and, you know, I always felt that I was very interested in managing money for people, so I just knew I could do that at some point. I wasn't interested in having surgery, which in those days was very rudimentary, and then hoping and praying that everything would be okay and that someone would sign me and everything would be hunky dory. I had seen too many guys that were operated on and didn't come back very well, and I just didn't want to sit around for two years and go through that. So, I just figured when I went home after '83, after spending six to eight weeks in the minors, that that was it. I went home and sent out my résumé to a bunch of brokerage firms and twenty-three years later that's what I am still doing.

*"Ted Williams, in many ways, shaped what I am doing today.
I'm what he called his legacy. We spent a lot of time together.
I got to know him really, really well,
and he became a good friend over the years,
so I was very fortunate to be in that situation."*

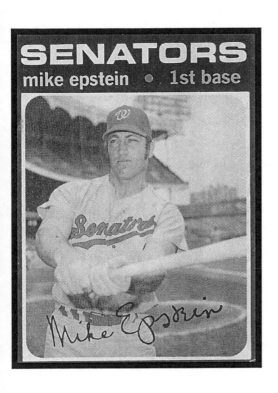

MIKE EPSTEIN

Mike Epstein *was born on April 4, 1943 in the Bronx. His family resided in Hartsdale, New York until 1957 when they moved west to Hollywood, California. At Fairfax High School, Epstein proved to be a very versatile athlete, playing both baseball and football. He was good enough, in fact, to play college baseball at the University of California-Berkeley, where in 1963 he hit .395 as a junior and was offered a contract by the Los Angeles Dodgers. It was not to be, though, as his father insisted that he stay and finish college. His first big career highlight came in 1964 when, as a collegiate All-American, he was chosen to be a member of the first U.S. Olympic baseball team that went on to win the gold medal in Japan. In 1965 Epstein began his professional career after signing with the Baltimore Orioles as an amateur free agent. His first assignment in the minor leagues sent him to the Stockton Ports in California. He would go on to earn MVP honors in the California League after leading the league in batting and home runs. In 1966, with the Rochester Red Wings, Epstein was named Sporting News Minor League Player of the Year as well as the International League MVP (.309, 29 HR's, 102 RBI's). In eight Major League seasons, Epstein played with the Baltimore Orioles, Washington Senators, Oakland Athletics, Texas Rangers, and California Angels. Highlights include playing for manager Ted Williams while with the Senators and winning the World Series with the Oakland A's in 1972. His best individual season was in 1969 with Washington when he hit .278 with 30 home runs and 85 RBI's. Owing to his religious background as well as his reputation as a power hitter, Epstein was tagged early on with the nickname "Super Jew." He played his final game on April 28, 1974 and now lives in Colorado, where he runs Mike Epstein Hitting, as one of the top hitting analysts and instructors in the nation. In 2003, he published a book on the subject,* Mike Epstein on Hitting.

You were born in New York and later your family moved out west to California. Tell me about those early years.

ME: When I was thirteen, my dad started up a West Coast office for the firm he was working with. In 1957 we moved to Hollywood, California, and I went to high school there and then enrolled at the University of California, so I spent a lot of years in California.

How was that transition of moving from the East Coast to the West Coast for you at that age?

ME: Well, you know, I didn't have a problem with it. I was okay with it because, and I've always been that way, it was just a new adventure. Once I got out there and saw how many people played sports because of the weather, to me I really believed that moving to California and getting into that kind of a highly competitive sports environment really fueled any desire that I would have had playing sports. It was a good move for me sports wise.

You were a good athlete in high school, playing both baseball and football. Were you a good athlete before you got to high school?

ME: I was. Even when I was living in New York, I could always throw a baseball really hard. I was really a pitcher then, but I could also hit. Then, when I moved to California, word got around that I could throw almost ninety miles an hour. Every scout that was in LA or that came out to LA wanted me to throw a bullpen session for them because they couldn't believe how hard one player could throw at that age. Unfortunately, I tried to accommodate them all, and I blew out that rotator cuff before I was sixteen. In those days there really wasn't anything you could do about it, so I wound up concentrating on hitting after that.

What kind of a household did you grow up in? Was it a "Jewish" upbringing?

ME: We belonged to a conservative temple in White Plains, New York, Temple Israel. I was bar mitzvah'd there. Once we got to the West Coast, the family got a little further away from religion ostensibly because the environment was different, the cultural environment, and so we weren't as religious out on the West Coast as we were in New York.

Were your parents supportive of your interest in sports, or were they like a lot of other Jewish parents, who stress getting an education and the unwavering desire that their son should grow up to be a doctor, a dentist or a lawyer? You know what I'm talking about.

ME: Actually, I don't think my parents really cared. You know, in those days it was a lot different than it is today where parents are almost expected to take a much more active part in their kids' lives, especially athletically. In those days people were, you know, the whole environment was different. I mean, we had parents earning a living, and they didn't have time for that. I don't think my parents ever saw me play a high school football game. I don't think they ever saw me play a high school baseball game or a college baseball game. They did see me play football once. They came up to watch when we played Penn State up in Berkeley, but I don't think my dad ever saw me play professionally until I got to the World Series at the end of my career. It was different in those days. The only thing that I can really remember about that is my dad did not want me to become a baseball player. When I was twenty-one and told him I was going to sign after I came back from playing on the first United States Olympic baseball team, he said, "I don't want you to become a bum like all the Major League Baseball players," or something like that. Sports were not really part of his life, so he didn't quite understand.

So for him, he obviously did not see baseball as a way to make a living and support a family. That was foreign to him.

ME: In fact when I got engaged to Barbara back in 1965, her father's family lived in Philadelphia and when they told them that Barb was engaged to get married, Barb's grandmother said to Barb's father, "From that he can make a living?" You know, as only Jewish people can say it. We always got a kick out of that.

In 1963, while you were playing at the University of California-Berkeley, you had a pretty good year. The Los Angeles Dodgers offered you a contract but, your dad said "no" because he wanted you to finish college first.

ME: Yes, my dad did not want me to sign. He said, "When you're twenty-one you can make your own decisions, but I'm not interested. I'm not going to co-sign with you." It never happened.

Do you remember how you felt about his opinion at that age of your life? I would imagine that you were not at all happy with his decision.

ME: I really didn't care. I mean, it wasn't anything that I really thought twice about. He said "no." I said, "Okay, I'll wait a year and see if somebody wants me." So I waited.

Hindsight being what it is, you made a pretty good decision because in 1964 you were a collegiate All-American. You were also a member of the first U.S. Olympic baseball team and were a part of that gold medal team that played in Japan.

ME: Yes, it was fun. It's funny how many players, I think, miss out today because they go after the dollars instead of the experience. I don't find anything wrong with it, but I think there's a lot of great life experiences that they miss.

Upon returning from the Olympics, you found out that there were still some teams out there that were interested in signing you. You ended up signing with the Baltimore Orioles. How did that come about?

ME: Actually, when I came back from the Olympic team, because I did well, and that was before the draft, there were a lot of teams that wanted me to sign with them. I just felt that I fit in better with Baltimore than some of the other teams that wanted to sign me because they had guys like Boog Powell, Jim Gentile, you know, some of the big hitters that I thought I could identify with. So I wound up signing with them.

How was your experience in the minor leagues? You started in Stockton, California but you were not in the minors very long.

ME: No, I wasn't. I was the Player of the Year in the California League, which was high A ball and then I was also the Rookie of the Year in that league. I sort of overmatched the league; it's just the way it happened I guess. The next year I went to spring training and I was ticketed to go to Double-A Elmira, New York, and Earl Weaver was the manager of Rochester. I guess he saw me play in a few games there and said, "I gotta have that guy," so they jumped me to Triple-A. It took me about thirty days to figure out what was going on and then after I did, I did well. I was the Rookie of the Year and the Player of the Year in the International League that year and also the Minor League Player of the Year. From then on I was in the major leagues. I was first called up for six games by the Orioles in 1966, when I was twenty-three. In the minors, I hit over .300 with at least 29 home runs and 100 RBI's in my first two Minor League seasons in Stockton and Rochester.

I read somewhere that, while you were in the minors, it was a former opposing team manager, Rocky Bridges, who gave you the nickname "Super Jew." Does he, in fact, get the credit for that?

ME: Yes, he did. I get a lot of bad publicity where people say I called myself "Super Jew." I never did that. I don't believe in that. I had hit a home run over the light tower in right center, and Rocky Bridges was the third base coach, and we had the third base dugout. When I was trotting out to first we sort of crossed paths, and he says, "You launched that one in the night, you Super Jew," and the clubhouse kid was picking up the bats around home plate at the end of the inning and he heard it. The next day when I came to the ballpark, he had Super Jew written over my locker and Super Jew written on my baseball equipment, so it stuck. I certainly never called myself that, and to me it just doesn't sound right, but those things happen.

At the time you didn't take it the wrong way?

ME: No, I didn't take it the wrong way. I took it as a real compliment, but I just didn't like the word. It didn't grate on me; it was just something I wished didn't happen. But, like I say, that's the way it's gone down, and some things in life you just can't change. Even in the *Encyclopedia of Baseball* that's what my nickname is.

I read somewhere as well that you used to draw the Star of David on your glove.

ME: I did. In fact, when I was inducted into the Rochester Red Wings Hall of Fame, they used a picture in which I have the glove in front of me. I'm wearing a glove, and my left fist is in the glove and you can see on the outside of the glove that there's a Jewish star on it, and that was something they thought was really neat. That's the picture they used on the plaque.

In 1967 you were traded from the Orioles to the Washington Senators. What were the reasons behind that trade?

ME: You know, I had a really good spring, but Hank Bauer told me the first day I got down there, he was the manager, he said, "You're not gonna make the club so don't get hurt playing." But I made the club and stayed with them until the cut down day which was the end of April, I think, or May 1st. They called me in, and they said they wanted to send me down. I said, "I didn't even get a chance to play here." In those days you didn't have any rights. Players just did what they were told and I just said, "Heck, if I'm here now, Boog is only a couple of years older than me." I said, "I'm not going anywhere." So I left. I didn't report, and I went home and actually I had told Harry Dalton, who was the general manager of the Orioles at that time, after a few weeks, he kept calling me and calling me and said, "Things change," that Boog might get hurt, and so on and so on. I said, "Harry, please don't call me unless you have something to tell me. Otherwise I'm just going to see an attorney and I'm going to see if I can do something about this legally." Two days later I was traded.

Do you think the trade to Washington was beneficial to you? Although it was a team that wasn't quite as competitive, you were going into a situation where you would be playing every day, and Ted Williams was the manager there.

ME: Well, not really. You know, Baltimore really had a good team. Frank Robinson had joined them and they really were a talented bunch. Over at Washington the game was approached entirely different. It was almost like an atmosphere of "Well, we'll go out and play and get the game over with because there are other things we want to do after the game." It was tough. It was a tough environment and we weren't going anywhere. The whole town was apathetic because the Senators really were pathetic. Then Ted Williams came in 1969. He was fun. He really injected a lot of energy into everything, and we responded to his enthusiasm, and we did well. It was the best year Washington had had in years. We even finished ahead of Baltimore that year. I think we finished third in the American League. And then in 1970 they broke up the team. The big trade with the Tigers, because Bob Short, the owner of the Senators, who shouldn't have had anything to do with the everyday activities of the ball club, he was in love with Denny McLain and he wanted Denny McLain. So he wound up trading most of our ball club for McLain. Gosh, we never recovered from that. Then Darold Knowles and I were traded to Oakland early in the following year. So it was tough playing in Washington, it really was. It was the big leagues and that was great; we played against the best players around. I loved the town, but it's always tough to play on a losing ball club. You have got to be a certain kind of player to do that.

I guess when I said that it was a good move for you, I kind of meant it in two ways. First, it gave you the chance to go somewhere where you were going to play a lot, and second, it gave you the opportunity to go to a team managed at the time by Ted Williams.

ME: In that respect you're right. It did give me the opportunity to play, and that was what I was looking for, and I was thankful for that. Ted Williams, in many ways, shaped what I am doing today. I'm what he called his legacy. We spent a lot of time together. I got to know him really, really well, and he became a good friend over the years, so I was very fortunate to be in that situation.

TED SHOWS HOW

MIKE EPSTEIN • TED WILLIAMS

In 1971 you get sent to Oakland. Looking back, you went from Baltimore, which was a team loaded with talent, to Washington, a team that struggled, to a flashy, World Series-caliber Oakland team. That had to reinvigorate your enthusiasm.

ME: Yes, that's basically right. We were all around the same age, and we knew each other from our college days, from playing. Some of the guys were from Southern California and I knew them and had played against them before my professional days, so it was an easy fit for me. My whole attitude changed because all of a sudden we were really playing for something. I had I don't know how many home runs I hit in the second half of the year. It was like twenty, and I remember Dick Williams making a quote that if it wasn't for that trade with Washington and getting Epstein, we would not have gotten this far, which was nice. The next year I led the A's in home runs. I had a good offensive year but got run down the last six weeks of the season and my average dropped from .320 to .270 by the end of the season. But I still led the team in home runs and some other hitting categories. It was great, and then we got to the World Series. My home run against Detroit got us into the World Series, and just playing in a World Series was unbelievable. It's once in a lifetime stuff, and to win, I got a ring to show for it and a World Series trophy. I mean, that's cool.

What was it like being with the likes of Jim "Catfish" Hunter, Reggie Jackson, Sal Bando and having an eccentric owner like Charlie Finley? It certainly had to be a fun and interesting environment to be in every day during the season. My perception is something akin to a West Coast version of the vintage '70's Yankees.

ME: Well, it was. You know, there was always something going on. They were just a really good group of guys. We all got along well. I know they write about the fights and this and that, and I could be wrong, but I can't remember anybody fighting against one another. The only person they really fought against or that got in fights all the time was Reggie, but Reggie used to bring that stuff on himself. But most of the time, we were a pretty close group, we really were. It was fun. On occasion I see some of those guys today, and we have a good time reminiscing.

Going back to that 1972 World Series, that was some series. There were six one-run games.

ME: The only blow-out was game six when we went back to Cincinnati. It was a great World Series, but you know, in those days things were different than they are today. I mean, guys could pitch and those pitchers were tough. Today, you know, it's a little bit different, it's a little bit more conducive with the smaller stadiums and the smaller strike zones and all that. In those days the fields were big and the pitchers could really bring it. They had a good pitching staff, and we had a terrific pitching staff, and it turned out to be a pitching and defense kind of World Series with clutch hitting.

Mike Epstein

In 1972, you had 26 home runs, which put you third behind Dick Allen and Bobby Murcer. With everything that has gone on in baseball in recent years, all the home runs hit by guys like Mark McGuire, Sammy Sosa, and Barry Bonds, what are your thoughts on why so many more are hit these days compared to when you were still playing? Since you're still involved as a hitting instructor, maybe you have some insight about this.

ME: Well, everything is better. You know, nobody ever talks about the balls. The balls are a lot different today than they were when we played. When I played before 1970, you could rub a crease in the baseballs; I mean they were really soft. It was pathetic. You'd hit balls a ton, and they wouldn't go anywhere, so there weren't as many home runs hit. They don't talk about the balls so much anymore because baseball comes out and says all the time, "We haven't changed manufactures, and they're still done with the same specifications," but they're not. Anybody that played in that era and has felt the balls today clearly can feel the difference. The umpire strike zones, for one, they're so small. They're postage-stamp size compared to what we had to contend with. We had pitches that were called from the armpits to the bottom of the knees, that was our vertical strike zone. It was a lot bigger than it is today. You know, today, you can sit on pitches and wait and wait and wait. It's like Billy Bean's philosophy at Oakland. Let's get rid of the starting pitchers by the fifth inning and get into the "not as good" bullpen. In those days you couldn't do it, they'd ring you up. That's made a big difference. You know, one of the things I don't understand is the players today are bigger and stronger than we ever were. I mean, the Minor League players, the big league players that we work with here, these guys dwarf me, and I was considered big for that era. I think what's interesting is that the current players don't hit the ball nearly as far as we did, and the ballparks are so much smaller. When I played in Oakland in 1972, even though I hit 26 home runs, I hit 18 balls that were caught with the right-fielder's back just about at the right-center field wall. It was 385 feet in those days. Today it's 362. You know, so the ballparks are a lot smaller too. Plus, the lights are better, the backgrounds are better. It's made a big difference.

So, you go from Oakland to the California Angels. What brought about that trade?

ME: The reason I got traded from Oakland was because there was an altercation in the clubhouse in Texas. Reggie was spouting off, doing dumb things and, anyway, I wound up going over and knocking him out. He was unconscious on the floor. Dick Williams was worried and they called the club owner Charlie Finley, and Finley got me on the phone and said, "I ought to trade you." I said, "Why?" He said, "You're the bad apple." I said, "I would think you that would go and ask the other guys on the team. The bad apple is unconscious on the floor in the clubhouse." He said, "No, he's not. I signed him. I traded for you. He's my boy. You're not my boy. I'm gonna trade you." So I said, "Go ahead and trade me. I've been traded before." He said, "I'm not going to trade you now. You're leading the American League in home runs and you're hitting way over .300." I said, "So you want your cake and you want to eat it too?" He said, "I always do." And right after the World Series was over I got traded, and they traded me back to the Texas organization because Bob Short wanted me back. He was the owner when I was traded and so they were in Texas. The Washington Senators had relocated to Arlington. I told Bob I didn't want to go back to Texas, and he said, "Oh, you're going to be my big guy and you're gonna be this and that." He gave me a good contract and a lot of money, but a week after I was at spring training he kept telling me every day down there, he says, "Finley keeps calling me. He wants you back. So how about trading you back?" I said, "Well I've got all my buddies over there." Anyway, as it was, the way the ballpark at Arlington was configured, the old ballpark, those winds used to blow out of the south at thirty miles an hour every night. I'd hit some trademark high fly balls to right field that would just get hung up in that wind, so Whitey Herzog says to me, "I gotta get you out of here. You'll be a basket case in another month." I wound up getting traded to the Angels for Jim Spencer. I played there for a while, but my heart wasn't in it. I was only thirty-one years old, but my heart wasn't in it. There were other things I wanted to do. I had done the things that I had wanted to do in baseball. I probably could have played for another eight or nine years and probably could have put up some really good numbers, but there were other things. I wanted to get on with my life, so I just decided that I was going to leave and I did.

I know you worked in the minors with the Padres and the Brewers. Did you ever have any desire to get into managing or coaching at the Major League level?

ME: Well, I was interested at one time but things have changed all through the years. One of the things that I just don't understand is when you have a guy like Ted Williams, who sixty years ago said all the things that were right about hitting, and then all of a sudden somebody, my ex-teammate Charlie Lau, comes on the scene, and he talks about a hitting philosophy that almost put baseball out of business in the early 1990's, you know, in the dead ball era. I have a little bit of a problem with that. People say Williams was the only one that could hit that way. Well that's not true because all the great hitters hit the same way. Ted had a great influence on me, and I was mentored by him, but once I got into the organizations and stuff like that, I found out that what was taught in the minor leagues, they did not even want to know about Ted Williams, they didn't care about Ted Williams. The whole hitting philosophy wasn't based on physics anymore; it was just based on throwing your hands at the ball. So, it wasn't a good fit. I helped a lot of players get to the big leagues, and they'd say, "Why doesn't anybody teach what you teach?" I'd say "Because there aren't a whole lot of jobs, and that's the way baseball is." So, I really didn't want to buck the system. It wasn't worth it to me. We just do, and I do, what I feel is right, and I just carry on the Williams tradition, and we've had a lot of success doing it. I had aspirations at one point, but baseball wasn't ready for change. Baseball's never ready for change. It's a very traditional oriented sport, so I just do my thing, and I don't have to worry about other people.

It's interesting to note that what I started doing at Williams' request back in 2000, in a span of seven years, is turning hitting around dramatically in the United States. It's almost like people are waking up and saying, "Hey, you know, Williams was right," which is a good feeling.

"On the day of Sandy Koufax's perfect game, Yosh Kawano, the brother of the Dodgers' clubhouse manager, walked me over to the clubhouse and I got to congratulate him and talk to him for a few minutes. When he found out I was Jewish, he whispered a 'Mazel Tov' and signed a ball for me, which my mother still has. He remains an icon in our family."

KEN HOLTZMAN

Ken Holtzman

Ken Holtzman's *first full season in the major leagues was Sandy Koufax's last. It was almost as if the mantle had been passed from one to the other, at least in the minds of Chicago Cubs fans and Jewish baseball fans looking to continue to root for "one of their own." The Cubs drafted Holtzman in 1965, following his graduation from the University of Illinois. After a short stint in the minors, Holtzman made his debut during a late season call-up on September 4, 1965. During the first month of his rookie season, on September 25, 1966, Holtzman faced Koufax one day after Yom Kippur. With his parents watching from the stands, he pitched a no-hitter into the eighth inning before eventually winning a two-hit 2-1 decision. It was the last regular season appearance for the future Hall of Famer Koufax. Holtzman would go on to win 174 games during his fifteen-year career, including two no-hitters. The first came in 1969, 3-0 over the Atlanta Braves, when he out dueled another future Hall of Famer, Phil Niekro. The second came in 1971, 1-0 over the Cincinnati Reds, the first no-hitter ever thrown at Riverfront Stadium. Although he may not have known it at the time, his career would take a huge upswing in late 1971 when he was traded to the Oakland Athletics. Joining an already established pitching staff of Jim "Catfish" Hunter, John "Blue Moon" Odom, and Vida Blue, and with the flashy Reggie Jackson's bat, the A's would go on to win the World Series three years in a row. He played for the Orioles and Yankees between 1976 and 1978 before New York traded him to the Cubs. He retired in 1979 with an overall record of 174-150 and an ERA of 3.49. Those 174 wins are the most by a Jewish pitcher, and he's second to Koufax with strike outs. After his baseball career, he found success in the business world in St. Louis, where he now works as a substitute teacher. In 1985 he received four votes for the Baseball Hall of Fame; in 1986, he received five.*

$$\diamond \quad \diamond \quad \diamond$$

While you were in high school and college, were your parents supportive of the idea of baseball as a career? Did you grow up in an observant Jewish home?

KH: My parents were supportive of my career from Little League to the major leagues. It helped that I got a scholarship to college because education was a bigger family priority than a future in baseball, so my parents were thankful that baseball made it possible and affordable. They were basically Conservative, but my grandparents on both sides were Orthodox, so I was bar mitzvah'd in an Orthodox shul. They later became more Reform but faithfully attended holiday services and were always involved in Jewish community affairs.

How exciting was it for you to be drafted by the Cubs coming out of the University of Illinois in 1965?

KH: I heard about it on the radio driving home from school after my last final in June of 1965. Waiting at my house was Vedie Himsl and Bill Prince who were scouts for the Cubs. They had a long talk with my father, and they assured him that Major League Baseball would pay for my continuing education through the graduate level in addition to the signing amount. Two days later I was on a plane to Boise, Idaho and my first professional team, the Caldwell Cubs.

You must have pitched very well in the minors since you were only there for twelve games. Your record was 8-3 with an ERA of 1.99. What other minor stops did you make?

KH: I probably had early success at my first stop because I was one of the few players who had played at the collegiate level, so I was quickly promoted to Wenatchee in the Northwest League which had many college players. It was ironic that I played against many of my future World Champion teammates of eight years hence because Lewiston was the Class-A affiliate of the Oakland A's, and they were in the same league as Wenatchee.

You were called up in September of 1965. Can you remember how exciting that was for you that day?

KH: The day I was called up I had to grab a bus to Spokane for an all-night flight to Chicago. The person who picked me up at O'Hare was none other than Buck O'Neil, who was a scouting director for the Cubs and who later became the central figure in Ken Burns' documentary about baseball on PBS. Buck is in the Negro League Hall of Fame, and it is to baseball's everlasting shame that he is not in Cooperstown. Buck drove me to Wrigley Field and introduced me to Ernie Banks and Billy Williams and all the other players. Needless to say, it was a very exciting day, and when I got dressed and walked out on the field for the first time, I was over-powered. It remains my biggest thrill, exceeding even all the World Series championships, the no-hitters, All-Star games, everything.

You made your debut on September 4, 1965. What were your thoughts as you pitched in majors for the first time?

KH: In those days, the Cubs had a rotating "college of coaches" system in which a different coach would assume the role of manager every few months. Lou Klein was the head coach when I arrived, and he told me that he would try and get me in a game, which didn't mean a lot. I thought that was kind of strange since the Cubs were about twenty-five games out of first place! Anyway, in about a week he put me in against the San Francisco Giants (we were getting killed that day), and I promptly gave up a home run to Jim Ray Hart. In fact, the first four hitters I faced in the majors were Jim Ray Hart, Willie Mays, Willie McCovey, and Orlando Cepeda. I called my parents after the game and told them I hope it gets a little easier!

In your first full rookie season you went 11-16. How tough was the adjustment once you joined the Cubs full-time in 1966?

KH: Leo Durocher, the new manager, had to decide in spring training if he was going to rebuild the franchise or string along with the old veteran pitchers who were still with the team. Thankfully, he decided to use the young guys, so Fergie Jenkins, Bill Hands, Joe Niekro, Rich Nye, and I were eventually made starters, even though all of us were in our early twenties and had no experience. For a team which lost over 100 games, my 11-16 record with a respectable ERA led the club, and I was made a permanent starter as a result.

We've all heard the stories of Sandy Koufax and Hank Greenberg not playing on the Jewish High Holidays. Did you ever come across a situation where you had to make a similar decision?

KH: I never played or even showed up to the park on holidays. I didn't make a big deal out of it, and I always discussed it with my managers well in advance, and they were very supportive. I was moved back in the rotation for the 1973 playoffs in Baltimore because of the conflict and pitched game three instead of game two.

On September 25th in 1966, you faced Sandy Koufax. That had to have been a big thrill for you. Was he someone you looked up to?

KH: The day I faced Koufax, my parents were in the stands, and it was the day after Yom Kippur, which means we both had to delay our starts for one day while we went to services. My mother, like all Jewish mothers, absolutely idolized Sandy. She couldn't bear to sit and watch so she walked around the park all day. Adding to the excitement was the fact that I had a no-hitter for eight innings and lost it in the ninth, but I got the win and it turned out to be the last regular season loss for Sandy, as he retired at the end of the year. I didn't get a chance to talk with him after the game, but he sent a note over to our clubhouse. Ironically, I had a chance to meet and talk to him the year before. In September of 1965, while on a road trip to Los Angeles, I pitched batting practice before the regular game because our players wanted to bat against a left-handed pitcher. That was the day of Sandy's perfect game and afterwards, Yosh Kawano, the Cubs' clubhouse manager, whose brother Nobu had that same job for the Dodgers, walked me over to the Dodger clubhouse and I got to congratulate him and talk to him for a few minutes. When Koufax found out I was Jewish, he whispered a "Mazel Tov" and signed a ball for me, which my mother still has. He remains an icon in our family. I spoke to him last year and he remains the classy gentleman that he always was.

In 1967 you spent time in the National Guard, appearing in only twelve games. You won nine of them. How difficult was that to shuffle between the two?

KH: I went in the service on active duty in 1967 and missed the next three months. When my basic training was over, I was sent to Fort Sam Houston for advanced training, and it was here that I was able to get several weekend passes to join the team and got to pitch in four games the remainder of the season. It seems that every time I showed up, the club would score a lot of runs, so I finished 9-0, which is one of the few undefeated records ever for a starting pitcher.

What do you remember about your two no-hitters? Your first came in 1969 when you outdueled Phil Niekro and the Atlanta Braves 3-0, and then in 1971 you blanked the Reds in Cincinnati 1-0.

KH: The first no-hitter in 1969 was during one of the most memorable seasons in Chicago history, and it was sheer bedlam every day at the park until we later collapsed in the end and the Mets overtook us and went on to win the World Series. I remember Hank Aaron making the last out and later giving me one of his bats that he had used. To this day it remains one of my prized possessions. The second no-hitter was two years later in Cincinnati and was the second game of a double-header. I remember I almost lost the no-hitter when Johnny Bench made a surprising bunt attempt which just rolled foul at the last moment and would have been an easy base hit. The last out of the game was Lee May, who I later played with at Baltimore and who became a great friend. I also got one of his bats!

What was your reaction at being traded to the Oakland A's in November of 1971? Did you, at that time, realize that you were going to a World Series-caliber team?

KH: My reaction to being traded was ambivalent since I had asked to be traded, and I didn't care where. When I was notified it was to be the Oakland A's, I did some quick research and discovered that they were division winners with a lot of young players, so I felt as if this was going to be a tremendous opportunity. Needless to say, this group went on to become one of the greatest teams in Major League history.

What a pitching staff you were a part of at Oakland! What was it like to be part of a staff with pitchers like Catfish Hunter and Vida Blue and "Blue Moon" Odom?

KH: I've often said that I didn't mind being the third-best pitcher on two terrific pitching staffs. There are three Hall of Famers (Jenkins, Hunter, and Fingers) and another who should be (Vida Blue). I believe we are still the last staff to have three 20-game winners and our post-season success has not been surpassed. I learned a lot from Fergie Jenkins and Bill Hands in Chicago, and they prepared me for later success at Oakland with Vida and Catfish. Before his death, Catfish and I were very close, and Vida remains a true and respected friend. I hope one day he is also voted in to Cooperstown.

Any interesting insight on having Reggie Jackson as a teammate? I did not remember until you mentioned it that you were with him in Oakland, Baltimore, and then New York.

KH: Reggie and I were teammates on three different teams, so I had the privilege of playing with him a long time. He is probably one of the most intelligent players ever to play and someone who I don't get to see very often. He remains a good friend. Reggie had a flair for the dramatic, and I know he is always stamped with the Yankees label. But he was a very important part of our Oakland team, and I'm sure if you ask him, will always attest to the ultimate greatness of our bunch in Oakland.

You were also teammates with Mike Epstein. Because there were and are currently so few Jewish Major League players, was there ever a feeling of camaraderie between you two?

KH: Mike Epstein and I became quite close, and we were together in 1972 when the Munich massacre happened. We both wore black armbands the next day, and I remember when I pitched that night, he joked that he wasn't going to be making any visits to the mound because one shot might get us both! I was with Mike two years ago at Cooperstown for a seminar, and he remains a true "soul brother" to this day.

When you, Mike Epstein and Reggie Jackson wore those black armbands in memory of the eleven Israeli athletes, do you remember what you were feeling during that time?

KH: It was during a trip to Chicago to play the White Sox when we started wearing the armbands. Mike and I didn't know Reggie wanted to wear one until we already had ours on, and he then expressed a desire to wear one as well. I remember discussing the situation with Mike and, besides being very sad, we were also a little nervous about making a public show of support.

The 1972, 1973, and 1974 seasons must have been an awesome time for you? What was it like to be a part of those great Oakland teams?

KH: Aside from just comparing statistics (and trophies), many baseball people that I speak to who are still in the game and those whose careers spanned the seasons from thirty years before and thirty years after, always maintain that the Oakland A's of that era were one of the three best teams ever. We had three Hall of Famers, a Hall of Fame manager, four others who one could make a case for being voted into Cooperstown, and a few others who, while not among statistical leaders, were very valuable players. Dick Green, the second baseman, was almost voted the MVP of the 1974 series and he went 0 for 15 at the plate! He saved so many runs with his defensive play that I told Rollie, who did win the MVP, that he ought to let Greenie use the car that he won on weekends!

In 1973 you won twenty-one games and were named to the All-Star team. What do you remember about your first All-Star game?

KH: The only thing I remember about the 1972 All-Star Game was that Nolan Ryan and I were the only pitchers on the American League team who did not see action. I remember telling him that since we had a lead going into the last inning, I was sure that he would be used as the closer, but he wasn't. We sat through the whole game and talked about everything but baseball, so I spent an enjoyable evening chatting with the strikeout king.

In April of 1976 you were traded, along with Reggie Jackson and Bill Van Bommell, to the Baltimore Orioles in return for Don Baylor, Mike Torrez, and Paul Mitchell. That must have been a very interesting time and maybe even a little unsettling for you.

KH: When Reggie and I were traded to Baltimore in spring training, we were shocked. First of all, we didn't want to break up the team which had a chance to win it all every year! We knew Finley wasn't going to pay higher salaries, but we thought he would wait until the end of the year and then let everyone go. I didn't mind, necessarily, being traded to Baltimore, but Reggie sure did, and he didn't report for about five weeks. Since Baltimore wasn't going to sign me (they knew I would ultimately become a member of the first class of free agents), they traded me to the Yankees in mid-season, and Reggie joined me the following year.

You were with the Yankees during an interesting time as well. What stands out to you about that time period in your career?

KH: Getting traded to the Yankees was both the best and worst event of my career. I eventually signed for what, at the time, was one of the largest contracts in baseball, and I also was a part of three more World Series teams. But I was hardly used and, eventually, I asked to be traded in order to salvage the few remaining years of my career with a team that could use an experienced starter. I'm grateful for the rings and the money but really it was not a very memorable time for me.

How was it to deal with George Steinbrenner? That was during the height of the Bronx Zoo, as Sparky Lyle called it.

KH: I never had a good relationship with Steinbrenner and the rest of the front office. Although I was a member of two more championship teams, I don't have many fond memories of New York.

Ron Blomberg told me that he never really heard many anti-Semitic comments when he was in New York. The only time he remembers anything was on one or two occasions while he was in the minor leagues. Did you ever have to deal with anything like that?

KH: It is a subject that I don't care to elaborate on. I will say that I experienced it at both the amateur and professional level, and it was not confined to fans but included players as well as people in control.

Blomberg also told me that, in a sense, he was placed on a pedestal as a Jewish Yankees player. He said he was often invited to Jewish children's bar mitzvahs, and birthday parties. Did you have any similar experiences in New York or Chicago?

KH: I experienced a very good relationship with the Jewish community and maintained that connection even after retirement.

The Yankees did end up trading you back to Chicago and the Cubs, and you ended your career with them in 1979. Talk about your post baseball career. You worked as a stock broker and in the insurance business.

KH: From 1980 to 1992, I was a co-owner of a business in Chicago which was involved in investments and insurance. I functioned as both an accountant and principal before I sold my interest in 1993. I then went back to DePaul to obtain a teaching credential and began teaching in 1995. In 1997, I moved back home to St. Louis to become supervisor of the St. Louis Jewish Community Center and remained there for eight years. Since then, I still teach, although this past year I've done more subbing because of some health problems. Hopefully, I'll be able to resume full-time teaching duties next year.

Who were a few of the toughest hitters you faced during your career? I read that Joe Torre had some success against you.

KH: Joe Torre was certainly, from a statistical standpoint, the toughest hitter I had to face, and I can't believe he is not in the Hall of Fame based on his playing record. I'm sure he'll be voted in because of his managerial success, but I think he has been mistakenly overlooked. Dick Allen and Orlando Cepeda were also two great players who I had a lot of trouble with and, like Joe, are certainly deserving of Hall of Fame status.

I grew up in the Boston area during the 1970's and followed the Red Sox. Looking back, I really think the 1950's through the 1970's were one of the best periods in baseball. Your career fell right in the middle of that time period. How do you think it compares to the mid 1980's and up, when the game became so specialized, expansion teams watered down the competition, tightly wound baseballs, smaller ballparks and, of course, steroids changed the game? I ask this as I see that you pitched 127 complete games during your career of your 410 starts. In today's game a complete game is considered a great accomplishment.

KH: Today's game, from an outsider's standpoint, is certainly more specialized and offensive-minded. When I played, pitching dominated the game in the sense that a good starting pitcher was expected to shut down the other team for the whole game and possibly three times in a seven game series. I never wanted to come out of a game, and that includes when I was with Oakland and had a Hall of Fame relief pitcher, Rollie Fingers, behind me. Even there, I used to have fifteen to twenty complete games a year. One thing I've noticed about pitching performance and evaluation today is that the strikeouts to walks ratio is considered an important stat, and a two-to-one ratio is the benchmark for an effective pitcher. The thing is that many great pitchers during the 50's, 60's and 70's didn't have a two-to-one ratio but were consistent winners. I'm thinking of Palmer, Hunter, and Drysdale. There are a lot of pitchers today who have a two-to-one ratio or better but also have very high ERA's and give up a lot more hits than innings pitched as well as having losing records. Forty years ago, a lot of them couldn't make a Major League roster with those stats. Also, the offensive mentality has changed as a lot of hitters today would rather strike out than cut down on their swing with two strikes in order to put the ball in play. This explains the high strikeout totals even among .300 hitters and high strikeouts to walks ratios among mediocre and poorly performing pitchers with high ERA's and sub-par records. Another consequence of this change is the slowdown of the game into too many three-hour marathons (even in relatively low-scoring games), which makes it hard to sustain interest on the part of the casual fan. That's why the new ballparks have incorporated so many more diversions and amusements for both fans and kids who have trouble maintaining their interest on a radically slowed down game with many pitching changes and high pitch counts.

In 2007 you managed in the Israeli Baseball League with the Petach Tikva Pioneers. Is managing something you had ever thought about? How was your experience there?

KH: I never wanted to be a manager or coach, but when I was asked to help launch the new Israel Baseball League I felt that it was a chance to see the country, and at the same time, impart some of my experience to some young players. It turns out that the experience was very unpleasant. Seeing the country was certainly very rewarding, and I'm glad I finally got to see the Israeli "Miracle" that I had heard about for so long. But the baseball part was very poorly run and the quality of play wasn't what I expected. If baseball ever succeeds in Israel, it won't be because of a few Jewish Major League players representing the country in the World Baseball Classic. It will necessitate a cultural change beginning with youth sports and will take many years and a commitment to prioritizing better facilities and personnel. I hope it eventually becomes a reality, but I'm afraid the odds are quite long.

Since the game was such a big part of your life, did you find it difficult to be away from the game when you did retire? Or, because you were formally educated and had post-career options, was it an easier adjustment?

KH: The only time I miss the game these days is when bad weather arrives in March and thoughts of a warm spring training keeps dancing in my head. I was comfortable with my retirement decision because I had prepared for that day and, yes, my educational background played an important part in the decision.

*"God I can't believe this is what I'm doing.
This is what I love, playing baseball. I get to do it and have all this fun.
Every day was baseball and they're teaching me.
The Dodgers were good.
They had a lot of lectures trying to teach you all about baseball.
It was a place that manufactured ballplayers. It was great."*

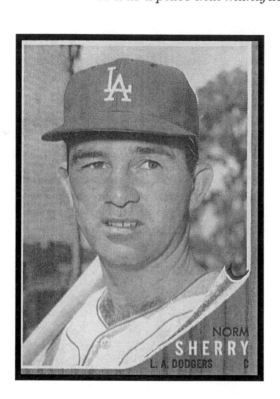

NORM SHERRY

Norm Sherry

Norman Sherry *was born in New York City in 1931, but the Sherry family later made their way to the West Coast, settling in Los Angeles. He attended Fairfax High School and, along with his two brothers, George and Larry, went on to become a Major League ball player. Norm signed with the Dodgers while they were still based in Brooklyn and spent seven seasons shuttling between their Minor League teams and two years of military service, finally reaching the majors in 1959. His brother Larry was signed by the Dodgers as well in 1953 but made it to the big leagues one year earlier than Norm for a "cup of coffee" in 1958. They were the tenth brother battery to play in the major leagues. Their other brother George spent a season in the Pittsburgh Pirates organization. In all, it was nine years before Norm reached the major leagues for good. He was twenty-eight years old.*

From 1960-1962 he was with the Dodgers as a back-up catcher. He may not have known it at the time, but he played a crucial role in the development of his friend and future Hall of Famer Sandy Koufax, working with him on his control issues and helping him to become one of the most dominant pitchers of his era. Diminished playing time culminated with the Dodgers selling his contract to the New York Mets in 1962, but after only 63 games and 147 at-bats, his Major League playing career came to an end on September 26, 1963, with a batting average of .215 with 18 home runs and 69 RBI's. In 1965 he transitioned to coaching and managing, beginning in the Dodgers organization and then, four years later in 1969, switching to the California Angels system. He did go on to become the manager of the Angels in July of 1976, replacing the fired Dick Williams. California went 37-29 the rest of the way that year, and the Angels brass brought him back to manage again in 1977. By that time they had added some big-name free agents such as Bobby Grich and Joe Rudi and were expected to contend, but following a 39-42 start, Sherry was released. His managerial record stands at 76-71 (.517). With baseball still in his blood, he rejoined Williams as a coach in Montreal with the Expos and then the San Diego Padres. His last coaching stop was with manager Roger Craig in San Francisco with the Giants. He now lives in San

Diego. His brother Larry retired at the end of the 1968 season with a record of 53-44, 606 strikeouts, 82 saves, and an ERA of 3.67. Larry went on to coach with the Dodgers, Pirates, and Angels organizations.

Tell me what it was like for you growing up. You were born in New York in 1931 but grew up in Los Angeles.

NS: Yes, I did. We lived in the Fairfax and Beverly area. It was all apartment buildings and mostly Jewish people.

Did you grow up in what would be considered a "Jewish" household?

NS: No, not really. My parents were not Orthodox or anything like that. We weren't very religious. I know I'm Jewish, but my mother and my father, even my grandparents were not very religious people.

You had two brothers who played ball as well. Larry was also drafted by the Dodgers, and George was with the Pirates.

NS: Yes, George played a year in the Pirates' organization but hurt his arm and he had to quit. He started in 1951; I guess that was the only year he played.

I'm guessing that with the three of you, playing sports was a big part of your lives during the time that you guys were growing up.

NS: Well, that's true. I was four years older than Larry, who was the youngest, and George was fourteen months younger than I, so we would always be playing together. We would get out back behind the house in the alley, and we'd pitch to one another and take turns being the pitcher and the catcher. The high school was about a half a block away, and we would go up there and play on their fields. We were always playing baseball with whatever kids were around the neighborhood, but my brothers and I usually played together more than anything.

While you were growing up, did you and your brothers ever talk about someday becoming professional ball players?

NS: Well, I guess so because I can recall to this day that when I was going from the second grade to the third grade, as the teacher is marching us out the door, she is asking every kid, "What do you want to be when you grow up?" I remember I said, "I want to be a baseball player." So I guess that at that very young age I really knew what I wanted to do, and I was very fortunate that I was able to play baseball.

As you played throughout high school, was there a certain point in time where you started to realize that maybe this was going to happen, that you would have a shot at making this a reality?

NS: I know that my senior year I did very well and our team in high school did very well. We won the city championship in Los Angeles. I was voted the best player in our league. I thought I was going to be the best player in the city, they always give a Player of the City and a lot of people told me I was going to be it, but it never happened. They gave it to a guy by the name of Paul Pettit, who the Pirates gave a big bonus to. At any rate, I wanted to play ball, but when I graduated from high school I had a scout come over to the house, but they didn't offer me very much money. I thought I should get a little bit more. At the time there was a bonus rule. They could give you $6,000, which included your salary. If you got over that you had to be one of the twenty-five guys on the Major League roster. Not many people got to be that pick, especially some kid out of high school.

What were your parents' thoughts on baseball as a potential career, not just for you but for you brothers as well?

NS: They were very supportive. My mother and father, my dad especially, loved sports. He would come to our games and my mom was like, "Whatever you guys want to do," because we always wanted to talk baseball, baseball, baseball, so she knew that's what we wanted to do. I had the opportunity. I was offered a scholarship to the University of Southern California, and I was supposed to go and start school on a Monday. But I signed a baseball contract with the Hollywood Stars on a Sunday night. I enrolled but I never actually attended USC. So yes, my parents were quite supportive.

Tell me about the process and timeline that ultimately led to your signing with the Dodgers.

NS: A friend of mine said they were having a tryout for the Hollywood Stars, who were a Triple-A farm club for the Dodgers at that time. They were having a tryout down at the ballpark, Gilmore Field they called it, so he says, "Come on, I'm going down there. You want to go with me?" I said, "No, I don't want to go." He says again, "Come on. Go with me." So I did go with the guy and they came after me. As the catcher I had a really strong arm, and they wanted to sign me. At that time, the manager of the Hollywood Stars was Fred Haney and the scout at the time, Howie Hink was his name, and he brought Fred Haney over to the house. I wanted to play ball in the worst way, so they talked me into signing and not going to school.

When you signed with the Dodgers, what Minor League team were you assigned to first?

NS: I signed with the Hollywood Stars, but I never got the opportunity to play with them. I started my first year in Santa Barbara in the California State League. That was my first beginning in professional baseball.

If you remember, what was your mindset as you left home for the first time and headed to Santa Barbara to begin your professional career? It must have been a very exciting time.

NS: Oh yes, it was. I thought, I get to play baseball every day and they are going to pay me? It was just something that I always thought that if I just kept playing and plugging along that good things would happen. So yes, I was quite excited to be able to go out and start playing baseball, that's for sure.

You spent seven years in the minor leagues. Do you remember all of the places that you played along the way to making it to the majors?

NS: Oh, of course. Like that first year I started playing in Santa Barbara and the next year I started in Fort Worth. Bobby Bragan was the manager and he was the playing manager at that time and, you know, I show up to spring training. Like I said, I had this terrific arm, and he really liked the fact that I could catch and throw and was not as concerned with my hitting, so he took me with him to Fort Worth, Texas in Double-A ball. I stayed there until almost the middle of June, and I didn't hit very much there. At one point they were thinking of making a pitcher out of me because of my arm. I wasn't hitting very well, but I caught a fellow by the name of Rex Barney, and Barney had come down from the Dodgers. He'd had trouble with all of his control, and he couldn't throw strikes. Bragan had twisted his ankle, so I got to play. I'm catching Rex Barney, he's wilder than heck, and all the scouts from Brooklyn are there watching him pitch. Bragan had told him, "The first time you walk three guys in an inning, I'm taking you out." He pitched seven innings and walked sixteen guys in this game. I was catching and I was jumping and diving. I was all over the place. They liked the way I could catch, and they just decided to leave me at catcher and hoped that maybe I would learn to hit. From there they sent me on to Newport News, Virginia which was a B-league, and I finished the season there. The next year I was going to spring training, that was 1952, and the day I got my tickets to go to spring training I got my draft notice and I went in the Army for two years. When I came out in 1954, I started in Fort Worth, Texas and gosh, I thought I was doing really well, but they sent a catcher down from Brooklyn so they make room by sending me back to Newport News and I played in Class-B again. In 1955 I played in Fort Worth the whole year, and that winter I had some surgery done on my back. Early in the season I had my elbow operated on, so I had a tough year that year. I went to spring training that next year, and my back was really stiff and I could hardly walk. I spent the whole spring trying to get treatments and trying to get to where I could walk a little bit so I could play baseball. They sent me to Fort Worth again while I was on the disabled list in 1956, and I stayed there until about June before they let me play. I got active one night and I played four innings. The next night I started and played five innings then they took me out. The next day they put me back on the disabled list saying, "You're not ready to play," which I couldn't believe because I really was, at that point, ready to play. Then they turned around and sent me to Buffalo, New York. I played Triple-A ball in Buffalo, and that was 1956 and then the next year was 1957. The Dodgers, at that time, had made a purchase of the Los Angeles Angels, the Pacific Coast League team. This was their in-roads to come to California, I guess, because they had that franchise. The Pirates now had the Hollywood franchise. So I took spring training with the Los Angeles Angels of the Coast League and had a very good spring. Again, a guy came down from Brooklyn, and they sent me to Saint Paul, Minnesota and where I played in 1957, and then in 1958 I played in Spokane, Washington, which was Triple-A and then, finally, I got a Major League contract in 1959. I was in spring training with the Dodgers, and I started the season with the Dodgers. We played in Chicago, and in the second game of the season I got a base hit and drove a couple of runs in. I might have gotten two hits, I can't remember, but, anyhow, we came back to LA and they said, "Joe Pignatano has no options and we'll have to keep him. You've got options, so we're going to send you back to Triple-A." So I went back to Spokane, completely frustrated. I thought that I had played well that spring and deserved to be in the big leagues. So that was my Minor League career at that point.

Boy, that's a good memory!

NS: Yeah, I got it all.

You mentioned that you finally reached the major leagues in 1959. Do you remember what it was like when you walked into that Major League clubhouse and then onto the field for first time?

NS: Well yeah, that was in 1959. You have to go all the way back to spring training. That was the first time I ever batted in a game, in spring training. The guys were like, "Why the hell don't you stop shaking?" I was so nervous. It was quite exciting. Then starting the season on the road in Chicago, and I got to play in that second ball game, yes it was thrilling. Being in spring training, around all those guys, you're not unfamiliar with them when you go into the clubhouse at the start of the season. I knew all these guys now. I'd been in spring training with them the year before too. All the guys from Brooklyn came down because that's the year Roy Campanella had the auto accident, and they brought a lot of guys in to see if they could find a catcher that could play in the big leagues. That first year, playing in that first game was really something because it was something that I was always wanted to do. I knew all those years that I played in the minor leagues that one day I was going to get a chance to play in the major leagues, and it happened.

Having been there a few times myself in recent years, I can only imagine what it must have been like in 1959 to go to spring training with the Dodgers down to Vero Beach. To be there with the likes of Duke Snider, Gil Hodges, Sandy Koufax, Don Drysdale, and all the other greats of the game that wore Dodger blue at that time.

NS: Oh yeah, that was a place. You go back to the very first year that I went there in 1951, because the first year, like I said, I played in Santa Barbara, California and they took spring training on the Pacific Coast out in Anaheim. That first year in Vero Beach, it was something to go down there and these guys, they had something like twenty-eight Minor League clubs at that time. They had around five hundred guys there, that's what it seemed like, and I looked around and said, "Everybody's walking around with a catcher's glove on. Where the hell am I going to play? There are so many guys here!" But they had, like I said, all these teams. It was really something because it was nothing but guys, and they're out there playing baseball all day long. In the evening you're sitting around talking. It was terrific. We stayed in those barracks with four guys to a room in bunk beds. It was like, "God I can't believe this is what I'm doing. This is what I love, playing baseball. I get to do it and have all this fun." Every day was baseball and they're teaching me. The Dodgers were good. They had a lot of lectures trying to teach you all about baseball. It was a place that manufactured ballplayers. It was great.

You and your brother Larry played together with the Dodgers. What was the first year you were teammates?

NS: Yes, in 1958 I started the season with the Dodgers, and he had a tough time at the beginning of the season but he'd had a good spring for them. They sent Larry up to Spokane, where I was catching, so we played together then. That winter we both went to Venezuela and played at Maracaibo. Of course, the next spring Larry began the season with the club, and then they sent him to Saint Paul, Minnesota. They brought him up in the middle of the season, and he did really well and that was in 1959. They brought me back at the end of 1959, so I was there with him. I got to watch him as he went from being a good pitcher to becoming better and better. Then he went to the World Series, where he won two and saved two games and they gave him the Most Valuable Player award in the World Series. That was really an exciting thing for me, to watch my little brother get so good so quick. It was like every day was a better game than the last one, and every situation a tougher one, and he rose to the occasion and did a terrific job. 1960 was the first full year that we played together in the major leagues.

When I researched your career, your relationship with Sandy Koufax is always mentioned, and it details how you helped him gain control of his fastball. What exactly did you do to assist him? Whatever it was, it certainly had an impact on his pitching.

NS: It's funny because I knew that Sandy had this great arm, but he could not always command his pitches, and control was a big thing. They sent us on this split-squad game over in Orlando. We went, and there was supposed to be three pitchers, but one guy missed the plane. I think there was just one other pitcher that went with us, and we had only nine players. We did not have a whole lot of guys when we went over there. On the plane going there he had talked to me about how he'd like to try and throw more curve balls and change-ups and work on those pitches. I said, "Sure, not a problem." So, when the game started, after we batted, we went on the field. Sandy tried to mix in these change-ups and curve balls, and he was having trouble throwing strikes. In fact, he walked everybody. Then he got a little upset at the last guy and he said, "The hell with this," and he's throwing all fast balls, and he's reaching back throwing each one harder and higher. After he walked the batter, I went out to the mound. I told him, "Sandy, we don't have any extra players. We'll be here all day long at the rate we're going. You got to take something off the ball and let them hit it and then that way we can make some outs. We'll hit some balls and we can get out of here." So I went back behind the plate and he relaxed, and I guess he said in his mind, "Hit the ball." He threw it over the plate, and he struck them all out. So now when he's coming off the field I ran to him and I said, "Sandy, I'm not blowing any smoke." I said, "But you just now threw harder trying not to than when you were trying to." I think he said that it really rang a bell with him and he changed his whole way of trying to pitch. He went on from there to become a hell of a pitcher, like the best one I've ever seen.

Koufax refused to play during the Jewish High Holidays. Did you ever find yourself facing a similar decision?

NS: No, because he was a superstar and people looked up to him. No, I did not. You know, I went to the ballpark and played. Well, I don't know if I ever played, but I was there. I did not observe the holidays like he did.

Did you and your brother Larry become friends with Koufax? Was there any feeling of camaraderie in that you three were Jewish ballplayers?

NS: I roomed with Sandy in 1962. Oh yeah, we were friends. You know, you are on the same ball club, you're going to be friends, and we were friends. You know, you get in that club house there and you're a ball player. Nobody thinks of you as being Jewish, Italian, or black or white or whatever. You're just a ballplayer. See, I never had problems. I get asked that question a lot and I say, "No. We were all friends. I didn't have a problem with anybody."

Unfortunately in 1961 and 1962 your playing time decreased, resulting in your average dropping to .256 and then .182. In October of 1962 the Dodgers sold your contract to the New York Mets. What was that time period like for you? Were you disappointed that you were leaving Los Angeles?

NS: Well, in 1962 I was standing in the outfield in Dodger Stadium and shagging during batting practice. I had new spikes on and the ground was very hard. Someone hit a ball to my left, and I went to get it, only my feet didn't turn and I popped my knee. The cartilage pumped up, and my leg swelled up, and I was limping around. I couldn't play. They did put me on the disabled list and I warmed up the pitchers. I put this one leg out and put all of my weight on the other and that one popped up, both bad knees, and I didn't do anything that year. I hit nothing. I was lucky to be there. They kept me there the whole year, and that winter they sold me to the Mets. I went to New York, and I still had problems with my knees, with the cartilage, and I didn't hit there either. Not to make excuses, but in baseball if you can't stay back and wait for the ball to come to you, you can't be chopping at the ball. I could not put any weight on my left leg. Every time I tried to it would come up and go forward and they'd get me out pretty easy because I couldn't stay back and hit the ball. So that was the end of my career in 1963 as far as being a Major League ballplayer. When they sent me to the Mets, I felt bad because I had been in the Dodgers organization for all that time, but that's baseball and at least I was still in the major leagues. I felt that was a pretty good break because the way I was I couldn't really do anything. I was hoping I would be in better physical condition when I went to New York but I didn't, the knee was still bothering me. The next year they sent my contract to Triple-A, to Buffalo, New York and my knee never bothered me, which irritated the hell out of me!

So you reach one of those so-called fork-in-the-road decisions with regards to your baseball career. Your playing days were over. So now what do you do?

NS: It's funny because I came home after the 1964 season, and I was looking for something to do. I had these friends downtown, and they set me up with this guy from JP Stevens. They manufactured carpeting, stuff like that, and I was going to be a sales rep for them in Los Angeles. They offered me something like a fifteen-thousand dollar salary, an expense account, and all this stuff. I said, "That's pretty good." I'd get to start in 1965, I guess it was. Buzzi Bavasi calls me and says, "What are you doing?" I said, "Nothing." He then says, "I need a manager in Santa Barbara." I said, "Really?" He said, "Why don't you come up and we'll talk about it?" So I went up and he said, "I'll give you six thousand dollars." I said, "I'll take it." Crazy! It might have been eight thousand dollars, I can't remember now. So I started managing for the Dodgers.

Eventually, after managing the Dodgers' Minor League club in Santa Barbara, you left the organization and caught on with the California Angels system.

NS: Well, what happened was I managed for three years there, in Santa Barbara, from 1965 to 1967. Then, right at the end of 1967, Buzzi says, "You know, I can get you a better job where you can get more money." As it turned out, the Yankees were looking for someone to scout the area, and Buzzi said, "You'll make more money doing that than I can pay you." So I went up to work for the Yankees in 1968 and I scouted in the Los Angeles area. By then, all the guys that I knew from the Dodgers had gone over to the Angels. I had four years of Major League time and needed five to get a pension, so I was talking to this guy with the Angels, and he said, "Listen, you come over here and work for us and we'll get you that next year so you can get your five years in." So, I quit the Yankees and went to work for the Angels. I scouted and managed the rookie team for them in 1969, and then they made me a coach in 1970. I was the pitching coach when Lefty Phillips became the manager. He was Jewish too. We were friends from way back. He was the first guy that came to my house trying to sign me. Anyway, he was managing the club and made me the pitching coach. I stayed there for two years until we all got fired, but I stayed in the Angels organization and managed at Double-A two years, Triple-A two years then I got to go as the third base coach for Dick Williams in 1976. He got fired in July and they made me the manager. They hired me for that next season, 1977, and they fired me in the middle of 1977. Dick Williams had gone to Montreal, so he called me and asked me if I'd like to come up there. They had this kid they wanted to make a catcher out of, and if I could work with this guy, you know, I could be the third base coach too. I said, "Sure." So I went to Montreal in 1978.

So in 1976, when Dick Williams got fired that July, how surreal was that for you to all of a sudden become the manager of a Major League club?

NS: That was really, really something, I'm gonna tell you. It was hard for me to believe. You're right, it was surreal because I had never thought of becoming a Major League manager. I just wanted to get my five years in, which I got, because then I could get some kind of a pension. But becoming the manager of the Angels was very exciting. I was on cloud nine. In a sense we did really well, I couldn't believe it. The club responded, and we finished up with a pretty good record. I'd finished with a good record as manager, so they re-hired me for the next year. They went out that next year and through free agency, they bought Don Baylor, they got Bobby Grich, they got Joe Rudi and Dave LaRoche. So they did a lot of things but, you know, I had trouble at the beginning of the year. Bobby Grich never did come to us in spring training. He hurt his back and had to have surgery, and Joe Rudi, in May, broke a bone in his hand. Don Baylor was having a tough year adjusting to being a DH. Other than Nolan Ryan, the pitching was not really that strong. We struggled along, and they just decided to get rid of me, and they did. At least I'd had a year doing it. It was quite interesting and fun and exciting.

You then went to Montreal to work on Dick William's staff. When the staff got fired there you ended up following Williams on to San Diego?

NS: Yes, we all got fired in Montreal in 1982 or 1981 and Dick had gotten the job in San Diego. He wanted me to be his pitching coach, so I went with him. We went to the World Series in 1984 and got beat by Detroit, and they let me go after that season. The next year Roger Craig got the managing job in San Francisco, and he asked me to be the pitching coach so I went up there for six years.

What did you do when your six-year stay with the Giants ended?

NS: Well, after the major leagues, I think 1991 was my last year as a Major League coach. In 1992-93 I managed a rookie team for the Giants up in Everett, Washington, which was like a part-time job. I worked June to September and then I retired after that. When they asked me, they said they weren't going to renew my contract, and I said I might as well retire so that's what I did.

So what have you done since then to occupy your time?

NS: I play a little golf a couple of times a week. There are a lot of ballplayers who live here in San Diego, so I play around with these guys. You know, time goes by. I can't believe I'm going to be seventy-seven this year. I don't do a whole lot. Every now and then I do a clinic, I've done some fantasy camps with the Padres, stuff like that, but not a whole lot of baseball stuff.

*"There are two Jewish Cy Young Award winners—
one was great and the other was me."*

STEVE STONE

To many baseball fans in Chicago and across the country, **Steve Stone** is best known not only for his seasons on the field, with both the Cubs and White Sox, but for his many years on television and radio as an analyst. Along with being one of only two Jewish Cy Young Award winners, he spent fifteen seasons with the legendary Harry Caray on the Cubs telecasts on WGN-TV and now can be heard on the White Sox television broadcasts. He is still regarded as one of the best Jewish pitchers in Major League history. Known by his teammates as "Stoney," his career spanned eleven seasons with four teams: the San Francisco Giants, Chicago White Sox, Chicago Cubs, and Baltimore Orioles. As a high school athlete in South Euclid, Ohio, Stone not only excelled on the diamond, but won several tennis championships as well as being better than average on the golf course. He went on to attend college at Kent State, where he was a teammate of future Yankees catcher Thurman Munson, another Ohio native. As a junior he was named to the All-Mid America Conference team as well as being named team captain. In 1968 he was drafted by the Cleveland Indians but elected to remain in school. He was drafted again in the secondary phase in 1969 by the San Francisco Giants. Stone graduated from college in 1970 with a teaching degree in history and government before beginning his professional baseball career.

After two seasons in the minors, Stone made is Major League debut with the Giants in 1971. He spent only one season there before being traded to the White Sox, where he also spent just one year before being sent to the cross-town Cubs. Following another short stint with the White Sox in 1977, Stone signed a four-year free-agent contract with the Baltimore Orioles. He enjoyed an All-Star season in 1980 when he went 25-7 while winning the American League Cy Young Award and the Sporting News Pitcher of the Year award. Arm troubles developed in 1981 and he went 4-7. He retired following the 1981 season, having played his last game on September 29. In 1983 Stone joined Harry Caray in the Cubs TV booth. After seventeen seasons on the Cubs broadcast, Stone resigned, and in March of 2008 he joined the White Sox radio broadcasts. In 2009, he moved to the White Sox television broadcasts. Stone is *the third-winningest Jewish pitcher, behind Sandy Koufax and Ken Holtzman. His career record was 107-93 with an ERA of 3.97. He recorded 1,065 strikeouts. Stone is a member of the International Jewish Sports Hall of Fame. He divides his time between Chicago and Arizona.*

Tell me a little bit about your early years.

SS: Well, I was born in Cleveland, Ohio and my parents were first-generation Americans. My four grandparents were immigrants. My father's parents were both from Russia and my mother's parents, her father was Hungarian and her mother was Polish/Czech and so they had lived through the pogroms in Russia and the beginnings of the Holocaust and the other events that many of the Jewish people of their generation and age group had to make it through. My father's mother was a child in a family of thirteen children. Between the pogroms of Russia and Hitler, they lost ten of the thirteen. Only three of the women made it, two coming to this country and one going to Australia. So getting that perspective from grandparents who were from the old country, I think, was an interesting way to experience what life was like for Jewish people at that time. My father was in World War II. He was a medic in the Army. I was actually fortunate just to be here because he was attached to a marine unit that was aboard a ship, and they were going to be the first wave of troops to invade Japan. Of course, Harry Truman decided to drop the bombs and when they did finally occupy the main island, they came in after the surrender had been accomplished. That was kind of fortunate because if you take a look at the odds of first waves of guys hitting the beaches, survival rates weren't particularly good. So, it was with that backdrop that I was raised with an Orthodox set of grandparents but a Conservative temple back round from my parents. I was bar mitzvah'd a couple of months after my thirteenth birthday and the temple we belonged to was a Conservative temple.

During your high school years, you were not only good at baseball but were a good tennis player and golfer as well.

SS: I was raised with an interesting background because it was my mother who was the great athlete in my family. I think I got most of my athletic ability from her, not that my father wasn't a good player of sorts, but my mother truly was an exceptional athlete. She was just over 5'1" and lettered in basketball in high school. I learned how to play golf with her clubs. There was a great female golfer at the time by the name of Patty Berg, and I learned how to play golf with Patty Berg clubs. My father had an old wooden Jack Kramer tennis racket, I believe. I learned how to play tennis with that. My father and mother knew each other from the age of fifteen on, and he told me that my mother was always the first to be picked when they played baseball in the streets. Both of my parents just loved baseball. My Hungarian grandfather was a phenomenal baseball fan. My Russian grandparents, I don't think, really understood how I could possibly entertain the idea of making this a career because they felt I should take advantage of all the educational opportunities that I had. But my Hungarian grandfather, Ed Mannheim, just loved the idea that I was playing baseball. In fact, my mother was very pregnant with me; this was July 13th of 1947. The day before I was born, my mother's father asked her, "Where you going?" because mother was getting ready, and she said, "I'm going to the baseball game." He said, "The baseball game? You could give birth at any moment!" She said, "Yeah, but Bill Veeck owns the team," and she said "If I give birth at the ballpark, I'm going to get a lifetime pass for my family and my child." At any rate, I was not born at the ballpark. I was born the next day, July 14th. Bill Veeck wound up being a very instrumental part of my career, but that's down the road. I was raised with that kind of background. That's how I started playing baseball, I guess. Just a love of it and very supportive parents.

You've been vocal with regards to parental support of kids and their sports activities and how it played a part in your life.

SS: Any time to this day that I go to talk to any groups that includes young players and their parents, I talk about supportive parents and how important it is in the development of their kids because that was really the case for me. My father, who was in the teamsters union and changed records in a jukebox, and my mother, who was a waitress, always had time to take me to whatever game that I was scheduled to play. They saw to it that that was the most important thing. It wasn't making money. It was being with the kids and raising us and certainly spending enough time with me. That was my background.

Was it in high school, from a baseball standpoint, that you really started to blossom into a player of the caliber that might be able to play beyond high school?

SS: Yes, I think so. Between my sophomore and junior years, I gained about three inches in height and about twenty-five pounds in weight and I, all of a sudden, started to throw the baseball a little bit harder. I was one of the few guys, I think, who made the major leagues as a .500 pitcher in Little League because I didn't have any fastball and I was really a midget. In fact, I was just over 5' 9," and starters of my size, even in my era, didn't do real well in the big leagues. I didn't know the odds against making it as a starting pitcher being sub-five foot ten and right-handed. I mean left-handers they would take at any height, right-handers were a bit different, but I didn't know the odds of that. I just figured and always have that there's going to be a contest that has a winner, and I couldn't understand, and nobody could explain to me, why it shouldn't be me. So, things started to get pretty good for me in high school, and I remember giving up two earned runs in my junior year and making all-state in my senior year, almost pitching my team to the state championship, but we lost. I had beaten this team from Shaker Heights, which was the wealthier kids around, many times in summer league ball, and we made an extraordinary amount of errors and I got hit pretty hard and knocked out. The first inning we came back from seven runs down. The last guy at the plate with the bases loaded in the last inning lined out. The second baseman made a leaping grab; otherwise we would have gone to the state championships and probably won. As it turned out Shaker Heights won the state title. The interesting thing about the state championships in Ohio is, number one it's a pretty big state and number two, every team played in the state championship. So you didn't have to win your league, you just went through a number of different teams and games, so it was truly a state championship. It was single elimination so the pressure was astonishing. It was during my last two years that I started on the varsity. The interesting part about my high school career was every game that I won, I didn't give up any runs and any time I did give up at least one run I lost the game, which for some reason we just never came back. I don't know my record. That escapes me at this point. I do remember that if I gave up any runs at all in any loss that I had, I lost the game. In every win that I had in high school I didn't give up any runs, they were all shutouts. I played in the Ohio all-star game and they broke the teams down to East and West and on my team, on the East, was me, of course, and Thurman Munson, who at that point, played shortstop and was really obnoxious, Larry Hisle, and Gene Tenace. We were all on the East of the Ohio all-star game, and we just killed the West three straight as you might expect.

And you thought that that Ohio all-star game would be the last time you'd have to play with Thurman Munson.

SS: Munson got beaten out at shortstop in the opening game, which is what everybody was shooting for, you know, to play that opening game. Munson got beaten out by a kid I played summer league baseball with that was from Cleveland by the name of Jimmy Redmon. I remember feeling really happy for Jimmy, and everybody was happy that Munson didn't start because he was just so abrasive. I mean, you know, people just didn't like him very much. Anyway, the three games are over and everybody is shaking hands and I remember Thurman walking up to me and he says, "Well, I'll see you in September." I said, "What are you talking about?" and he goes "I'm gonna catch you at Kent." I said, "You're the shortstop," and he goes, "Nah, I'm a catcher. I just didn't want to catch down here." But he says, "I'll see you in September and we're going to have a great time," and I went "Oh, my God." You know, I thought that I was done with this guy. At any rate, we turned out to be really good friends and we roomed together on the road.

Were you recruited to play at Kent State or were you planning on going there anyway?

SS: I was initially recruited under false pretenses actually, and it's made kind of a unique interaction since then. The coach has since passed away. I had very bad grades in high school but actually really good test scores on the aptitude tests, the college entrance tests that you had to take. So, I got accepted to Ohio State, which is where I really wanted to go. I fell in love with it and Marty Kurrow, their baseball coach, said, "We have enough pitching." I took particular delight in starting for Kent State the first game as we beat them in a doubleheader the year after they had won the national championship. That being said, Dick "Moose" Paskert, who was the coach at the time, said, "You know, if you come here I can't give you any money now, but if you come here and you prove yourself in the classroom I will get you a scholarship." Then I said, "Okay, that's fair," and I passed up going to Ohio University under Bob Wrenn, which put out Mike Schmidt and a few other real good ball players along the way, Bob Brenly being one of them. They had a really good baseball program. So I went to Kent State under this promise and had a 3.15 my first quarter and I went in and put in on Moose's desk and he turned gray. He looked at it and he goes, "Well, I guess I've got to tell you I was lying to you." He goes, "I really don't have any money. I gave it all away. I had no idea you could do it in the classroom." It wasn't that it inspired me as a college player, but that particular attitude of "We really don't think you can do it," is something that probably was a great incentive type situation my whole life. Being the size I was and doing the things that I wanted to do, a lot of people telling me along the way about what I couldn't do, and, so I just set out on a continuing basis to prove them wrong. I had a lot of help on the way, played with some wonderful players and for some great coaches. I had probably the most encouraging set of parents that anybody could have without being, you know, those people that always pushed you to do something. My father would never really tell me what to do. What he would always say is, "I'm going to tell you the right thing to do and then you make a choice, whatever you want to do." He really meant that. It was to go on to be a recurring theme throughout my life and certainly my career.

You graduated in 1970 with a teaching degree in history and government. What were your plans at that point?

SS: Right. The only reason I graduated in 1970 was because I went to play a year of pro ball in 1969 and unlike a lot of people, you know, there are some guys who just walk away from the educational aspect of it, but I knew the odds of making it. I knew how slim the odds of making it were as far as making it to the major leagues. I'm not talking about being a professional because there are a lot of professionals who never see the light of day in the major leagues and so I wanted to make sure that I got my degree. After my first year of baseball, the Giants' farm director, a guy by the name of Jack Schwartz, said he wanted me to play winter ball after I pitched a year at Fresno. I said, "Oh, I can understand that." I can understand where you'd want me to play winter ball." He replied, "Well are you going to do it?" And I said, "No, of course not." He said, "Well, what do you mean?" I said exactly what I'd said, "I'm not going to play winter ball. Let me ask you a question. If I blow my arm out are you going to take care of me for a couple of years until I get back on my feet and get this education and get started in some career?" And he goes "No." I said, "That's right, so I have to go back and do my student teaching and get my degree with a quarter of student teaching and one more quarter of school and then, you know, I'll make it when I make it." He goes, "Well, we think you can make the major leagues, but we have no idea when you're going to make it or if you're going to make it if you don't play winter ball." I said, "Well, then let me tell you. When I started this thing I gave you guys four years. You've just had one of them. If I don't make it in four years I'm going home so you can go on any time table you want to, but that's my time table, and I've got the deciding vote." So, that was it. After two years they invited me to spring training as a non-roster player. It was Juan Marichal and Gaylord Perry. I was the third starter. I made the team as a non-roster player after two years in the minor leagues and never did go to winter ball even to this very day. So, that's how that worked out.

You were actually drafted twice, the first time by the Cleveland Indians in 1968. At that point, did you know you were going to stay in school?

SS: Actually, no. Munson had invited me to Cape Cod to play in the Cape Cod league, which as you know is a great league, and we were going to have a wonderful team up there. Thurman said he was there the year before in Chatham, with a guy named Joe Lewis, and he said this would be great. We'd dominate the league; we'd have a lot of fun on Cape Cod. It'll be wonderful. Well, Munson's drafted number one by the Yankees, and we had a pitcher by the name of John Curtis, who was drafted number one by Boston and an infielder you might have heard of by the name of Bobby Valentine, who was drafted number one by the Dodgers. Another infielder named Rich McKinney, who was drafted number one by the White Sox and me, who was drafted number sixteen, sixteenth round by the Indians. So they all signed. So I'm left here with nothing. They all signed. Munson got a hundred and ten grand, Curtis got a hundred, Valentine got sixty-five, McKinney got thirty-five, and I got mono and hepatitis, spent the year in the hospital and in bed! So that's how that worked out in the summer of 1968, and then I got drafted in the winter draft of 1969 and then, it sounds really glamorous because I was drafted by the Giants in the fourth round, but seeing as they only had four rounds, and they released the first three guys, that's how that worked out. But I wound up making it after that.

How was Minor League ball for you during the 1969 through 1971 seasons?

SS: I loved it. I learned some valuable lessons. Nobody really believes it any longer, but I was the hardest throwing pitcher in the San Francisco organization, and the first half of my first year I was 3-10 with a 6.30 ERA, but I was averaging twelve strikeouts a game. I had some people that I had met in Bakersfield who were great fans of the Dodgers and, of course, the Giants were their mortal enemies. I happened to meet them one day while I was charting because one of our pitchers forgot their uniform, and I had to give him mine. At any rate, I met them and they were phenomenal fans of Sandy Koufax and, of course, he was my hero too so they gave me a book either co-written by him or about him. But in the book they asked him, "What's the most important pitch in baseball?" Koufax said, "You're going to get a lot of arguments from a lot of different people about the curveball because nobody really hits that or the well placed fastball or the changeup or the slider." But he said, "The best pitch in baseball has been and always will be strike one." And he said, "It sets up a defensive at-bat." Allen Roth apparently was a statistician and he said. "Allen Roth told me when I had a hitter 1-2, they hit .119 on me." Now granted, not many hitters hit Sandy very well at any count, but it really hit home with me that I wasn't concentrating that much on the first pitch and that every guy that wasn't striking out was hitting a double, so I completely changed my pitching philosophy because of Sandy Koufax and that one sentence, as well as reading the book of course. I went from 3-10, I won nine of my next ten and I wound up taking my 6.0 ERA and dropped it down to 3.60. The next year I went to Double-A and Triple-A and went 14-8. I think and that led to the invitation. I did not go to any rookie league or the low minors. I went right from the California League, a hitter's league, to the Texas League, a hitter's league, the Pacific Coast League, a hitter's league and averaged nine strikeouts a game. I went to my first Major League camp and struck out 38 men in 37 innings. Because I threw harder than everybody else, they were saying, "The next Sandy Koufax, the Giants have the next Sandy Koufax," only he's right-handed and he's small so that was that. It didn't turn out that way but I always tell people that one of the great trivia questions is "Who are the two Jewish Cy Young Award winners in baseball history?" And, of course, they know one of them and I always say that "One of them was great and the other one was me." So it worked out pretty well, actually, and it wouldn't have worked out that way without a wonderful team in Baltimore and some great experiences along the way. Things work out the way they are supposed to work out.

Do you remember how excited or nervous you were going into that Giants clubhouse for the first time as a member of the club?

SS: Well, you know, going into spring training, I just remember the smell of the cut grass in the morning, going there and taking a look at Willie Mays and Willie McCovey, Juan Marichal, Gaylord Perry, and Bobby Bonds. That team that won our division in 1971 before the Pirates derailed us to get to the World Series. My first Major League win, I shutout Pittsburgh in Pittsburgh and my folks were able to see that game. Yeah, it was thrilling. I mean, look at the guys I was able to play with. How many people can say their first Major League team they played with four Hall of Famers? Not too many.

Then you get traded from the Giants to the White Sox. You're a young player at that point. What was that like for you to be traded so quickly, after the one season in San Francisco?

SS: Well, it showed me everything I wanted to know about baseball because after that first year I couldn't really stand my manager, Charlie Fox, who also has passed away. I wasn't just one of those guys that just lived, ate, and slept baseball. I read books and had thoughts and all of those things, and Charlie thought that was somewhere close to being a Communist. At any rate, after my first year I went and talked to the general manager, and I asked him if he would trade me, and he said they would try and accommodate me but he didn't trade me. My second year I had a 2.98 ERA, and the general manager called me in the last month of the season and asked me if I still wanted to be traded, and I said, "You know what, I've grown up a lot and I've learned a little bit more about the game. You know, I think I'd like to stay here in San Francisco." So he said "Okay." I played in a golf tournament with Hank Sauer, who spent, I think, the greater part of thirty some-odd years in the San Francisco organization. We were at this golf tournament in Carmel, California, and Hank was playing with me and we sat down afterward, had a cocktail and Hank said, "Kid, they tried to trade you last year but I told them you're going to be a good pitcher one day and I want you to know something." I said, "What's that Hank?" He said, "As long as I'm with the Giants you're going to be right here." I said, "That's great." Ten days later I was traded to the Chicago White Sox. Hank spent the next thirty years there, I spent another nine days. As my partner Harry Caray would say, "That's baseball."

You were teammates with Ron Blomberg for a short time while with the White Sox.

SS: I was. I played with Ron. Ron was fine. Ron ate more than any human being I've ever seen.

Over the course of our interview you came across to me as someone who understands why it's important that we recognize Jewish players and how important it is to tell their stories. In the overall scheme of things, there have not been a lot of professional Jewish athletes period. The joke has always been told that book of Jewish athletes is actually a pamphlet. To some of the players I interviewed, it seemed that it was not that important to them.

SS: Well then, for some of the other guys maybe it isn't a big deal. However, I am very much a student of history. I read about it. It was what my degree was in. I realize the struggles that our people have gone through in many different eras, in many different countries, at many different vocations under very different circumstances would lead one to probably consider that someone from our religious group would always get the benefit of the doubt and would almost be, oh,

I would say you'd have a certain amount of simpatico with them until they show you otherwise, as has been the case at times with various players that will remain unnamed. It's just something that, if you understand anything about the struggles of the Jewish people through history, and then realize, number one, what a select club Major League Baseball is to begin with, and then you narrow it down to the miniscule population in this country and the odds of making it for any Jewish person, like I say, I feel an immediate bond. It's one of the reasons that led me to invite Shawn Green out for breakfast never having spoken to him or knowing him when he came in as a Los Angeles Dodger that first trip. I didn't know if he would even agree to do it, but I figured, you know what, I want to find out about Shawn Green because he was truly one of the stars. I was really never a star. I had a great eighteen months and a couple of other good years. I wanted to find out from his perspective what it was like. We had some really interesting conversations about the various pressures on him being in Los Angeles. He told me something that I couldn't believe somebody would say, and it showed me that he really had his whole life and his priorities in exactly the place they should be, which showed me that he had a pretty strong upbringing and a very good sense of himself. He said to me, "Sometimes I wish I didn't sign a contract for fourteen million a year," and I said, "That's the first time I ever heard that." And he said, "No, because with it came a lot of expectations and a lot of responsibilities simply because of the number I signed for." He said, "I was a very comfortable person with what I made in Toronto before I ever went to Los Angeles." So, at any rate, the rest of what we talked about are things that will remain between Shawn and me, but I always said "hello" to him after that. We did never go out to breakfast or lunch again. I felt it was an imposition on his time, and I didn't ever want to feel like I was imposing on anybody, but I think it was incumbent upon me to, number one, meet him and two, exchange some of our upbringing in the game and a number of other things. He's a very nice fellow, again, with a good sense of self. You know, he took a lot of heat that time for sitting out the night game and then playing the next day on, I believe it was Rosh Hashanah. It was one of the two major holidays. A lot of it came from the community but some of it, of all people, came from Steve Lyons. I mean what a ridiculous thing for a non-Jewish guy to say. First of all, everybody's religious belief is his own, and it's really nobody else's business but theirs, and if he decides to play on that day then that's his decision, that's his belief. If he decides to take a night off without the day off, then that's his belief.

What did you do with regards to playing on the Jewish High Holy Days?

SS: I, along with Sandy Koufax, because he was my hero, never pitched on either of the major Jewish holidays. I never pitched on Rosh Hashanah or Yom Kippur but I did only take one day on Rosh Hashanah and, of course, Yom Kippur and that was not as much for my religious beliefs as it was out of respect for all of those who preceded me, including of course my grandparents who had seen some of the horrors of the persecution of the Jews up close and personal. So, I just think it was out of respect for my predecessors and what they had gone through to get me to this point where I was able to play Major League Baseball. I'm not a supremely religious person.

So let me jump ahead here a little bit. You were telling me about the great season you had with the Orioles in 1980 and that you retired following the 1981 season.

SS: I actually had a great year and a half if you want to go back and count. I was undefeated from July 6th in 1979, didn't lose a game. After a pre-All-Star break confrontation with Earl Weaver, I did not lose another game that 1979 season. That covered thirteen starts. Then I went 25-7 in thirty-seven starts so I made fifty starts from the middle of 1979 on through 1980 and I lost seven times. That's one of those Koufax-ian numbers that I really should have never had but did that routinely. For that eighteen month period there was something special.

Did you retire following the 1981 season?

SS: Actually no. That's not it. I retired on June 2nd officially. The irony of my retirement was I decided on May 31st of 1982 after never getting off the disabled list that year because of elbow problems. I sat in that chair after a workout, having taken two cortisone shots in my elbow a week apart and not really getting any relief. I went in to Hank Peters, who was the general manager then, and I told him, "I can't help you anymore." He looked and he turned around and he picked up the medical report that says you're probably going to have to have elbow surgery or suffer with chronic tendonitis. I won't get into the specifics of it, but that was what the deal was and so, that night I took my uniform off, never to put it on again. It was the night that Cal Ripken started his all-time consecutive games played streak, May 31st 1982.

So now your career has ended. Little did you know at that point that you would be able to transition from the field to another baseball related career like you did? The broadcast booth.

SS: No, I didn't leave to go anywhere. I couldn't pitch any longer the way I wanted to. I could have hung on for a couple of years and been really mediocre and had lots of arm problems and wound up with arm surgery I guess, or taken cortisone shots or a number of other steroid-related drugs at that point. For me it was quality of career not quantity. I just felt it was time to close that door. I stayed unemployed for five minutes because as I walked out of the interview room, the secretary of the Orioles came up to me and she said, "You had two phone calls. David Hartman wants you to be on *Good Morning America*." He was a friend of mine and knew that I could speak because, quite obviously I had been interviewed a lot in the Cy Young Award year, and she said that Chuck Howard of ABC Sports called. Her words were, "I think he has a job for you. Call him first." So I called him first and he said, "Keith Jackson is going on vacation. Would you like to do a couple of games for us in the middle of June?" I said "Sure, of course." Because, you see, that was the brass ring. It's two months out of the game and it's going to be Steve who? I just figured, you know what? I'll go on the air. I didn't have any experience with it but the worst that could happen was I look like an idiot in front of thirty million people. I had no idea at the time who I was working with. Later he said, "We can get you a third game but it would be in four days and it would be in Montreal and I know you haven't been in the National League for, like, six years. Would you have any problems with that?" I said, "Chuck, I'll do Japanese baseball, just put me on the air." That's exactly what I told him, and so I found myself four days later in Montreal with Al Michaels and Don Drysdale. I had a two-game contract, and then the second game I worked with Al Michaels and Howard Cosell and then they extended it another game to Atlanta. Don Drysdale and I got rained out of that one, and then they gave me a contract for the rest of the year and the year after that. So, what started out as a two-game contract has turned into a twenty-seven year broadcast career. It's worked out pretty well.

You've obviously had the pleasure to work alongside some of the legends of broadcasting, including Harry Caray.

SS: I would say that I don't know if there's any guy who's worked with more play-by-play guys than I have. I would number them in triple digits. I don't think there are many analysts that could probably say that. But between the stroke that Harry had and the guest guys in the booth and working for all of the people that I worked for CBS, TBS, ESPN, ABC and all the guys that have come in and out of the various booths for WGN, Fox Sports Net and on Comcast and all of the things that I've done, yeah, I'd say it's been terrific. I've loved just about all of it.

How special do you view the time that you worked with Harry Caray on the Cubs broadcasts? Caray was a legend and a beloved broadcaster in the Chicago area.

SS: It was like a marriage. You have your good times and you have your bad times. You have your very difficult times; you have your very frustrating times. But at the end of the day, a very good marriage like a very good partnership has many more good times, many more entertaining times, many more enlightening times than bad ones. I learned a great deal from him. He was a most unique character, never to pass this way again. His style of broadcaster was legislated out of the game and, you know, some parts of it probably for the good, most parts of it probably for the bad because he was the greatest salesman of the game of baseball that ever lived and the greatest salesman of Harry that ever lived. Plus, he could sell beer also so if you needed a great salesman and the Cubs in 1983, actually 1982 when they brought Harry over, they brought Harry over in 1982, they brought me over in 1983, and he was the best salesman of baseball that there was and turned out to be a great salesman of the Cubs and Wrigley Field and the city of Chicago.

When you look back at your life and career, you have a lot to be thankful for with regards to the game of baseball. You made it to the top as a player and have managed to stay with the game as a broadcaster all these years.

SS: What I would say is that, number one, baseball has been my life, continues to be my life and I would say at the end of the day that it is probably summed up by one quote that Jim Bouton made in the book *Ball Four* many years ago when he talked about Jim O'Toole. O'Toole was a former pitcher for the Cincinnati Reds, and Jim Bouton was watching him pitch for a semi-pro team in some league somewhere in Kentucky (Kentucky Industrial League) and it was called the Ross Eversoles. Bouton said, "I wondered as I watched Jim O'Toole pitching for the Ross Eversoles if, when it was over for me, if I would be on a team very similar to that somewhere?" Then he said the answer came crystal clear, "You spend a great deal of your life gripping a baseball and in the end, and it was the other way around all the time." And that to me summarizes what a hold the game has had on me. It got me through my childhood, it got me through my adolescence, through my high school years, my college years, and I've been fortunate enough to be involved with professional baseball all of this time. The one thing that has remained consistent, even though the teams have changed, my job description has changed, certainly I have changed from the early years to the developmental years, the one thing that has remained consistent through all of those years has been my love for the game of baseball. It certainly does not supersede my love of family and dear friends and, of course my wife and the animals that we have been fortunate enough to have in our lives, but baseball has been my constant companion since as long as I can remember, since probably I was five years old, six years old, something like that. I really haven't been away from it. I've always had at least a radio show or multiple radio shows when I wasn't doing daily baseball, and hopefully that will never end. In a way you kind of have to admire what happened with Harry in that he was a broadcaster for the Chicago Cubs. Even though he passed away in February, he was looking forward to the next year as he looked forward to every other year, but he was still broadcasting baseball when he died. I knew it would never be during the baseball season because he would never have allowed that. So, there's something to be said for someone who's still doing what they're doing, what they love to do, of course the latest example we've had is Tim Russert, who actually passed away at work doing what he loved to do. Not a lot of people get to do that. I am one of the fortunate ones.

"It was just an unbelievable feeling at the time being nineteen, and here they are, opening day playing the national anthem, and I'm standing there with a Major League team. It was hard to believe."

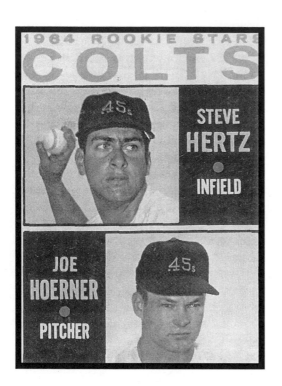

STEVE HERTZ

Steve Hertz *was only eighteen when he signed with the Houston Colt .45s as an amateur free agent in 1963, and in 1964 became the eighth youngest player, at that time, to reach the major leagues. He was nineteen when he broke spring training camp with the Colt .45s and headed back to start the regular season with the club. Born in Fairfield, Ohio but raised in Miami, Florida, Hertz knew early on that baseball was his passion. He was a pretty good player in high school, good enough to earn All-City and All-State honors while at Miami High School. What he did not know in the spring of 1964 is that he would appear in only five games as a Major Leaguer before being sent down to the minor leagues, never to return. In those five games, Hertz had four at-bats, from which he scored two runs. He spent five seasons in the minors, including being a member of the 1969 Tidewater Tides, the New York Mets' Triple-A farm team that won the International League Championship. Always mindful to complete his education, Hertz would return to Miami during each off-season and eventually earned his college degree from the University of Miami. Knowing that baseball would forever be a part of his life, Hertz embarked on a successful coaching career that began at Miami Coral Park High School, where he amassed 300 wins as well as winning the Florida State Championship in 1978. Following his time in the high school ranks, Hertz moved on to head coaching job at Miami-Dade College, where he has won more than 750 games and on six occasions been honored as Miami Coach of the Year. In 1987 he served as the head coach of the South squad at the United States Olympic Festival, guiding that team to a silver medal finish. Hertz also co-coached the U.S. entry in the Junior Pan American Maccabiah Games in Mexico City in 2001 as well as the games in Chile in 2003 with both teams winning gold medals. When Israel decided to try to start a professional baseball league in 2007, Hertz and a few other former Major Leaguers, including Ron Blomberg and Ken Holtzman, signed on to manage the teams. Hertz guided the Tel Aviv Lightning through a 26-14 season and a second-place finish.*

You were born in Fairfield, Ohio but actually grew up in Miami, Florida.

SH: I was born there because my father was stationed at Wright-Patterson Air Force Base at the time. My family is from St. Louis. I grew up in Miami, where we moved when I was a year old.

You were an All-City and All-State player in high school. What was it that fueled your passion for baseball?

SH: Well, I guess because I was pretty good at it. It's like anything else, if you're pretty good at it that's what you do.

Were your parents supportive of your passion for baseball and your desire to play at a higher level?

SH: My father was an athlete, so yes. My mother was supportive, too.

Tell me about how it was that you came to sign with the Colt .45s right out of high school.

SH: It came about where my last year in high school I had signed a scholarship to go to Rollins College in Winter Park, Florida and wound up playing in the summer league with what was called the Dodgers Rookies. It was made up of a lot of ex-professional baseball players, guys that were really good. I don't even remember how I got the opportunity, but I got a chance to play with them during that summer and did real well. There seemed to be a lot of scouts that would come to the games, and at that time there was no draft, so you could sign as a free agent. During the summer the Dodgers came in and made a real good offer, and I was about to sign with them, but then the Colts called and said, "You know, we'd like to give you a work out for Paul Richards." He was their general manager at the time. I did it, but I did not really plan on signing with them because I pretty much told the Dodgers I would and they had made the nice offer. But after going out to Houston and having a fantastic workout, the Colts made a much better offer than the Dodgers and, again, you could sign with anybody so I signed with the Colts that summer.

So you're eighteen years old and you've signed a professional baseball contract. I can only imagine how exciting that must have been for you.

SH: It was the best. And then, of course, I wanted to go to school too, and they were paying for school. So in the bonus I also got schooling, so I went to the University of Miami one semester a year. It took eight years to graduate, but I would do that September through December, go to spring training, play the season, comeback and go to school. Certainly it was well worth it, and they paid for the whole thing.

What was it like for you that first time you headed to spring training with the Colt .45s?

SH: Well, it was just a great opportunity. Fortunately, for whatever reason, I got a chance to play with the big team a lot during spring training and had a real good spring training. I'm not sure why, but I did. I think one of the reasons was that Bob Aspromonte was the third baseman for Houston the year before in 1962, and he came off of not a bad year but not a good year, and I think they used me as a way to push him to do better and so I was kind of competing with him at third base during spring training, which made him better. He seemed to really be concerned about me, the fact that I was doing well, but there was no way they were going to keep a high school kid or a rookie on the big league team. He had a great spring also and wound up as the third baseman for the Colts that year and had probably his best year in 1963.

Do you remember what other players were on that team? Was it intimidating to be around all of those Major Leaguers that you'd heard of?

SH: Well, that year they had Pete Runnells, who'd led the American League in hitting with the Red Sox but he was in his later years. Eddie Kasko, an outstanding shortstop, he was also one of the veteran guys that Houston took to steady the infield along with Aspromonte at third. You had Rusty Staub at first base, Jimmy Wynn in center field, Jerry Grote and John Bateman were the catchers. Pitchers were Turk Ferrell and Don Nottebart. There were guys that were pretty good those years. They had just gotten Nellie Fox from the Cubs.

Did you play at all with Larry Yellen?

SH: I did. We were both rookies that year in 1964.

So you break that first spring training with the Colt .45s. What happened at that point?

SH: Well, it was a surprise. About a week before spring training, Paul Richards came and said, "We're going to keep you with the big club." You know, it floored me because I thought I was going to Durham, in the Carolina League, that was pretty much what they had said. He said, "We've decided to keep you and don't plan on playing a lot," but with this new rule, you had two or three bonus guys over a certain amount of money, you had to keep one of them physically on the Major League roster. At the time there were two other ones, I think Walt Williams was one and John Paciorek, an outfielder from Detroit was the other one, and they wound up optioning them out and keeping me, at least the first couple of months. So I broke spring training with the big club and opened up the season in

Cincinnati, which again, you're right, that was just an unbelievable feeling at the time being nineteen, and here they are, opening day playing the national anthem, and I'm standing there with a Major League team. It was hard to believe.

I'm sure you remember the first time you ever went up to bat in the majors.

SH: They made sure I remembered it. The paper next day in Houston said, "Hertz boots big chance, Strikes out swinging." I didn't get too many at-bats so I remember a lot of things.

You only appeared in five games. What happened at that point?

SH: After two months Paul Richards came in and he says, "We're going to bring John Paciorek up from Durham. Not that he's going to sit here like you are." He says, "He needs an operation but we are going to physically put him on the roster. He'll have his back operation and this will free you up and you can go out and play every day," which is what I did.

So when it was all said and done, you had four at-bats, three strikeouts but you scored two runs. How did that come about?

SH: We'll, two reasons. One, I hit what I thought was a double to right-center against the Cubs. Lou Brock was the right fielder, he went over and it went off his glove, and they wound up giving him an error. I've been trying to change that for forty years, but it still goes as an error! Anyway, I'm on second base and wound up scoring, and then I went in to pinch run one time in Philadelphia and scored.

After getting sent down, you then spent the next five seasons in the minor leagues. Where were the different places you played?

SH: Cocoa Beach in the Florida State League, Salisbury in North Carolina, Durham, North Carolina, High Point, North Carolina, where I played for Jack McKeon, he was a manager in the Carolina League then. I wound up hooking up with him when he became the manager of the Marlins again thirty years later, and then Tidewater in Virginia with the Mets' Triple-A team.

You won an International League title while with Tidewater.

SH: Yes, I was lucky to be with that team. I was in the Florida State League with the Pompano Beach Mets, and there were a couple of months to go in the season up in Tidewater and they were fighting for the pennant. They had a couple of infielders hurt, and they asked me if I wanted to go. I'd be the utility infielder filling in here and there or I could stay. I was kind of a player-coach that last year with the Mets in the Florida State League. I said "Yes" and so I wound up going to Tidewater, not playing a lot but on that very, very good team which won the International League pennant.

When you're in spring training with the Colt .45s and thereafter in the minors, did you ever experience or encounter any negative situations being a young Jewish ballplayer?

SH: Nothing to speak of. There's no outstanding event or situation that really happened. You know, you'd hear some rumblings once in a while in the minor leagues, maybe some racist remarks occasionally, but nothing really to speak of.

During your time in the minor leagues, you were still very conscious of the fact that you needed to make sure that you finished your college education. You played during the season and then went back down to Florida to take classes in the off-season. You were basically working year-round.

SH: Well, if you call that working. Did I take school seriously like I should have? No. Did I do enough to get by and get a degree? Yes.

Early on did you know that you wanted baseball to be a part of your career path whether as a player or as a coach?

SH: Yes. I mean, I thought I might go into coaching when I was finished playing.

Sometimes former players make good coaches and sometimes they don't. What was it within you that led you to believe you would make a good coach?

SH: Well, I mean I didn't know that at the time. All I know is that I really like working with kids and trying to help them maximize their talents. From what I learned over the years, I thought I could relate to kids, and I thought it would be an enjoyable job, coaching baseball and teaching. And it has been.

You got the high school baseball coaching job at Coral Park and did very well there, winning 300 games. Tell me about your success there.

SH: Yes, I was lucky. I went into a well-established program. You know, we kept it going for about ten years, won a state championship there. Moved on to another baseball school that already had a good reputation, South Ridge High School. I took over a pretty good program there and kept that going for about five years. We did well there and then I had the opportunity to go to the community college here at Miami-Dade in 1986, and it was time to do that.

You've had a nice run there too, winning an average of 35 games a year.

SH: Yes, it's been good. Again, there was a great foundation coming in and we've just tried to maintain it.

You've also been fortunate to coach a number of players who have gone on to play in the major leagues.

SH: Well, going back to high school, Orestes Destrade, who now does some speaking on ESPN, I coached him in high school. I had Orlando Palmiero, who just finished his career in Houston, played about ten years in the big leagues. In junior college, I had Jaime Navarro, who played with the Cubs and White Sox. Omar Olivares with the Cardinals, Padres, and Pirates. Placido Polanco's been there about ten years having just a great career.

You also got the opportunity to coach in the Israeli Baseball League. How did that come about and what was the experience like?

SH: Well, it was the brain child of a businessman from Boston, who put the whole idea together to bring baseball to Israel and have a professional league there. I think his reasons for it were to give Israel something other than constant thoughts about war and anxiety and problems everyday and show them the national pastime and see if it could catch on.

Did you think that it was something that could develop?

SH: I don't think so. I was hoping it would. It was a great first year. There were some financial problems at the end of the year in 2007. They tried to resurrect it again in the summer of 2008. It didn't really work financially.

Had you ever been over there before, and if not, what was that experience like?

SH: It was just an amazing experience. You know, everyday you didn't know what was going to happen, a new step and a new adventure everyday trying to find three fields to play on, three venues, six teams. Just putting the whole thing together was a monumental task for the administration part of it. To make it work for as long as it did was something else. We all lived at the same hotel for two months in Tel Aviv. That was a great thing at that time to do that.

This is a Glass Half Full, Glass Half Empty question. Given that you were only in the major leagues for a very short time, do you see your career as a success because you were actually able to "make it" to the big leagues, or was it disappointing because you were there for such a short time, or both?

SH: Without a doubt, I've looked at it that way for a long time. The glass was half full, most of my life really, being able to experience that. The other half would be, you know, was I too young to really understand it? Was I in awe of the situation? Yes, if I was probably more mature at the time, had a better focus, maybe I would have been able to stay longer, I'm really not sure. You understand what I'm saying?

Yes, I do. While reading about the career of Hank Greenberg, he mentioned that it wasn't until after his career was over as a player that he realized just how special it was to be a Jewish Major Leaguer. Have you ever looked at it from that standpoint?

SH: No, I didn't at that time. But even so, it was a "Cup of Coffee." It's nice to be included in the group of Jews that have ever played in the big leagues, and it's nice to be included every time they have an event or have anything to do with that. You look fondly on it now, but then I look back too, what more could I have done to have had more of an impact and stayed in the big leagues longer and played more?

*"My only interaction with big league ballplayers before I went
into baseball happened when I was fifteen years old,
when I went to Ebbets Field. I went into the locker room after my
workout and I saw Jackie Robinson."*

DON TAUSSIG

Don Taussig

Many young baseball fans growing up in New York in the 1930's and 1940's dreamed of playing for the Yankees, the Giants, or the Brooklyn Dodgers. That was the case for a young **Donald Taussig***. Born in New York in 1932, Taussig developed into a pretty good player in high school and was good enough to play college baseball at Hofstra on Long Island. Taussig's dream became reality, albeit briefly, when he was signed by the Yankees as an amateur free agent prior to the 1950 season. But he never actually wore the pinstripes. Prior to the 1951 season, he was sent to the New York Giants. He did not know it at the time, but he would not take the field in a Giants uniform until 1958, by which time the franchise had moved to San Francisco. In 1952 he entered the armed services where he served for two years during the Korean War. Following his time in the military, he returned to the minor leagues, spending the next few seasons in places like Sioux City, Iowa and Dallas, Texas. He made his Major League debut on April 23, 1958 with the Giants when he had one at-bat against the St. Louis Cardinals. He would go on to play in 39 games with San Francisco, where he was a utility outfielder, playing behind starters Hank Sauer and Willie Mays. In 50 at-bats, he would amass 10 hits with 1 home run and 4 RBI's. Little did he know it at the time but that would all the action he would see with the Giants. In April of 1960 his contract was purchased by Portland in the Pacific Coast League. Then, prior to the 1961 season, as part of a Minor League working agreement, he was obtained by the St. Louis Cardinals, where he would enjoy the best season of his career. Taussig played in 98 games getting 188 at-bats. By the end of that season he hit .287 with 54 hits, including 14 doubles, 2 home runs, and 25 RBI's. In October of 1961, to his dismay, he was drafted by the Houston Colt .45s in the expansion draft. He would play in only 16 games for the Colt .45s, with 1 home run and 1 RBI before being drafted yet again by the Milwaukee Braves in the 1962 Minor League draft. He was assigned to the Braves B team in Toronto, where after just two weeks he was given his release, having played his final game on August 11, 1962. He now lives in Jupiter, Florida. In 2008, he published* Baseball: The Balanced Hand Method of Hitting.

Do you remember when you caught the baseball bug?

DT: Well, I probably started the game at the age of ten. I was playing slow-pitch softball. I would wake up at five and go down to a place called Fireman's Field. About forty guys would show up at five-thirty or six o'clock in the morning and we'd divvy up for games and the winners stayed on, it was a round-robin. Usually we had about three or four teams; it was a lot of fun. We played until lunch time. So, that's the way I started my baseball career or softball, I should say.

Did you start to get serious about the game once you reached high school?

DT: Yes, I did. What happened was, we only had twelve games every high school season. I played about twelve games but I used to go during the summer, I would travel to New York, the Polo Grounds, to Ebbets Field and to Yankee Stadium whenever the scouts there were holding tryouts. I started doing that when I was fifteen years old. I just enjoyed going in there and, you know, showing off for the scouts a little bit.

After high school you went on to college at Hofstra. How did that come about?

DT: Well, I had a football scholarship to Rutgers University, a full scholarship. It was wonderful, but the summer before I went to Rutgers, in one of the tryouts after I had graduated, the Yankees offered me a bonus and so I signed with them. But I had already made plans to go to Rutgers and signed with the Yankees about three weeks before I was supposed to go, so I went to Rutgers though for about half a semester and when I went to the football coach to tell him "I'm sorry, I'm a professional because I signed a contract with the Yankees, they gave me a bonus check." He said, "Sorry to lose you," and all that. I really wanted to play football. I called my father from Rutgers and said, "Look Dad, give them back that money, give them back their bonus. I want to play football here." My dad told me that I might mess up my knees or something in football and then I'd never have any kind of chance in baseball, so he talked me out of it.

You must have been awfully excited to be so young and to have signed with the Yankees being that you were a New Yorker.

DT: Oh yes, DiMaggio was always my hero. Because of him, I always wanted to play center field. I remember in my high school days I always used to watch the center fielders for all the New York teams. I loved Duke Snider of the Dodgers and DiMaggio and Bobby Thompson of the Giants. I loved Pete Reiser of the Dodgers, but he got hurt slamming into a center field wall so his career was short.

Center field was always my favorite position and it was very exciting later on in life when I got to play center field professionally. I loved it.

Once the Yankees had signed you as an amateur, where did you go from there?

DT: They sent me to Independence, Kansas. I went there and I had a contingency type of bonus where I got half for signing and then half on July 30th if I were still with the ball club. But my hitting habits were very poor. I think I had a very slow bat at that time. I had very bad habits at the plate, which came from having played slow-pitch softball. When it came time for them to give me my bonus, I got released the day before because I was hitting about .200. I hitched all the way back to New York by truck and car and whatever ways. Then I got hooked up with the Giants because I knew Bob Trocolar, a scout for the Giants, and I told him that the Yankees released me. He said, "Come on down and we'll send you to a college league up in New England to finish out the season." So, I signed with the Giants and then sent me to St. Johnsbury, Vermont, and that's the way I started with the Giants. I came up through the minors my whole career with the Giants.

Once you joined the Giants organization, where were you assigned to?

DT: Well, that following season I went to a "B" level team in Sunbury, Pennsylvania, that was in the interstate league and I hit about .250 there. Played a little bit of center field, left field, right field, I was all over the outfield and then the following year, if I remember correctly, I was drafted into the Army. When the Korean War started, they drafted a lot of ball players. I got drafted, I believe it was in 1952, and I spent two years in the armed services. I had put in about two or three years of Minor League ball by then because when I started out I was eighteen in 1950 so I was about twenty-one, I think, in when I got drafted into the Army. When I got out I think I went to Sioux City, Iowa and Dallas, Texas. I moved around the minors for four or five years before I went up to the big leagues and that was with two years spaced during the Korean conflict.

Your first year to reach the majors was 1958. How well do you remember that experience?

DT: 1958, yes. The year before I had learned how to hit, but I didn't know why I hit because when I would go through early preparation up till then, I had a bad habit of starting my movement late. I didn't realize I had a bad early movement but, you know, in slow-pitch softball, the way I was brought up, you start your movement as you see the ball, and in high school you can start your movement a little later because you're facing seventy mile an hour pitches from guys who aren't really throwing too hard. The guys who can throw hard, that means over eighty-five, ninety and ninety-five, if you start your movement too late, you'll never be on time for the ball, so I was working with those very poor habits, those inefficient habits. I did three or four years in the minor leagues and nobody ever really tried to correct it. The coaches would say different things. What I did was I changed my stance more than change my style. In other words it was just trial and error and that never worked. However, when I learned early preparation, because we were facing a fast-baller, he was throwing about ninety-five, from Shreveport, Louisiana, I remember this day, and a couple of guys would discuss it in the locker room saying that, "Boys, we have to start our movement a little earlier because this guy is very fast, if you want to be on time." I had tried it before, this early movement before the pitcher releases the ball, but I tried it probably in a tense state of mind and it never worked, it always just completely mixed me up. But this one day I concentrated a good deal, I practiced it against our starting pitcher before the game and then I practiced it quite a bit during the game. I was practicing it in the on-deck circle, and I managed to be very much on time and I hit two home runs that game. From then on, after discovering this early preparation, my confidence grew and I became a good hitter. I got a good feel in my hands and I finished the season with about 23 home runs, something like that, and almost a hundred RBI's with a .285 batting average. If the Giants had called me up right as the season ended I'd have been fine, but they gave me the contract in January of 1958, they sent me a big league contract. I was very happy about that, but meanwhile I had a reason for my success. My hands were strong enough at that time of the season, it was the midseason, so that when I tried this new move of early preparation, I had a good concentrated relaxation. The concentration of it relaxed me and that's what started me off. From then on I was a hitter, but when the season ended, they didn't call me up. I went back home and didn't swing a bat for three or four months, so all the strength that had been built up during the season in my hands just dissipated away and it was like starting over from scratch when I went to spring training in 1958, my first season in the big leagues.

Going back to 1950 when you signed as an amateur free agent with the Yankees, did you ever go to spring training with them? Did you have any interaction with any Yankee players?

DT: No, my only interaction with big league ballplayers before I went into baseball happened when I was fifteen years old, when I went to Ebbets Field. I went into the locker room after my workout and I saw Jackie Robinson and all the guys, and they were just, you know, Jackie Robinson, I can still picture him walking to the shower. He took a shower because he worked out before the game so he wanted to take a shower before the game, and he was walking pigeon-toed to the shower. It was amazing experience for a fifteen-year-old kid. My high school football coach, who was the New York Giants football pro, introduced me to Sid Gordon of the New York Giants at that time. Sid Gordon was a Jewish ball player, and my coach introduced me to him when he took me to a tryout at the Polo Grounds. That was a nice experience too.

So when was the first spring training you attend with the Giants, what was that experience like for you at that age?

DT: 1958. Tremendous. It was absolutely great. Even though my confidence level wasn't as good as the year before, I managed to hit well enough to break camp with the team. They played me enough in spring training because they were looking for guys who could rip the ball, hit the ball hard, you know, hit home runs. Whenever Willie Mays took the day off or something, I was in there in center field, so it was a pretty happy spring training for me. I hit well enough to go with the club but I didn't play. Once the season began, I did not play. I sat on the bench. I played in about 39 games that season and most of it was filling in defensively for Hank Sauer in left field or somebody else. Once in a while, I would play against a left-handed pitcher, but I only managed to get up to the plate around 50 times with 10 hits and 1 home run. That was my first year in the big leagues in 1958.

What was it like in that locker room with the Giants at that time? Little did you know that you were playing with some future Hall of Famers.

DT: On that team they had Orlando Cepeda, Willie Mays, Mike McCormick, the pitcher, Jimmy Davenport was the third baseman, Willie Kirkland was the right fielder and he was a left-handed hitter. Mays was, of course, in center field. We had a good ball club. We just didn't have the depth in pitching.

So what happened to you following the 1958 season?

DT: In 1959 they brought me back. They gave me a spot with a big league contract, but they optioned me out of the system during spring training. They optioned me to a cub team for the season, and I felt pretty bad about that because I thought they didn't want me anymore. There was nothing much to that season, and then I decided that I didn't want to play with the Giants anymore. I just didn't want to be in the organization anymore. I felt kind of neglected a little bit. I didn't really get a good shot. In 1958 they made room for me when they brought up a kid named Leon Wagner and another left-handed hitting outfielder who was hitting very well in Phoenix, and they sent me down to Phoenix and I started playing regular right in the middle of the summer. That was around July 15th I think, or late July. I tried to get started, but my timing was no good at the plate and I failed miserably, I think.

Then the Cardinals acquired you in 1961 and that turned out to be a turning point for you.

DT: Well, the turning point was when I got away from the Giants because I then went with Portland. In the last week at spring training, I was still at home, and then they said, "Don, we just sold your contract to Portland, Oregon in the Pacific Coast League," so I said, "Fine, I'll report." I went out there, and in a week's time I worked real hard at trying to get in shape and I had a very good year. I hit .286 with about 23 or 24 home runs and I had a 101 RBI's. One of my home runs was in Omaha against Bob Gibson and at that time Harold Walker, who would be the future coach of the Cardinals the next year, was the manager of the Omaha Cardinals, and when I hit the home run off of Gibson, he remembered me from the Texas League too because he was managing the Houston Cardinals when I had my good year with Dallas. So, I think he was instrumental in getting me to the Cardinals that next year because they were looking for a center fielder at that time. The year at Portland got me another shot in the big leagues.

You played in 98 games in 1961 with the Cardinals.

DT: Right, that was a wonderful, wonderful year. The big difference, why I was a good hitter that year, was because they invited me down to early spring training before the main roster of players came in. It was myself, two weeks early, and the pitchers and catchers. The pitchers and catchers stayed on one side of the field and I went on another side of the field. On my side there was an Iron Mike Pitching Machine, and I had two weeks of just swinging the bat against the pitching machine. I swung until my hands were bloody red and I loved it. I loved it because we didn't have any pitching machines in those days. We didn't have a lot of things where you could practice your swings in those days, during the off season. We just got in shape during spring training. When I got the opportunity to take those two thousand swings, that got my hands so strong that the feeling that a lot of ball players get, that the bat is an extension of their hands, which gives them the tremendous control and tremendous bat speed, I got it. I got it early. During spring training, when they put me in games, the pitchers couldn't get me out. I was hitting line drives. If they did get me out, it was a line drive right at somebody's glove. So they signed me to a contract in April. They were trying out their center fielders one at a time, and the young kid's sticks didn't start hitting, and they were sent out and they started to platoon me against left-handers, that's how I started my play with the Cardinals. By July I saw some newspaper articles that my parents had gotten, but I was leading the league in hitting. I was hitting about .360 and leading the National League but I didn't have the amount of at-bats necessary to qualify for the title. Most of the hitters on that list had twice as many at-bats as me. Johnny Keane took over for our manager Solly Hemne, who would only put me in against left-handers. We had two All-Star games that year, one was July 11th and one was July 31st, and between those games, Keane said to me, "Don, you're my regular center fielder from here on out," and when he said that to me I went bezerk inside. I mean the butterflies and everything, my dream had come true. I was going to get a starting shot in center field in the big leagues and I was like a little kid. At that time I was twenty-nine years old but I was so excited. This was my last chance to make it in the big leagues, and the butterflies were overwhelming. I described it in my book. It actually almost paralyzes the reflex action. There was one time during a game with the Los Angeles Dodgers, and

Johnny Podres, a left-hander, was on the mound, and I could see him pretty well and I was never bothered by Podres, I could hit him pretty good, but that day I was completely out of whack with my reflex action and I saw the ball pretty well, I saw his ball like it was as big as a softball when it was coming in, but when I swung, it was already in the catcher's glove so that's how much off my reflex action was. But I managed in the first at-bat, I managed to, after he got two strikes on me, he decided to work on me with curveballs and I got a little piece of a curveball, dribbled it down between the pitcher and the first baseman and beat it out for a base hit. So there I was, one for one, in the worst shape I think I'd been in in my career. The second at-bat was even better because it was the same procedure. He got ahead of me with two strikes because of fast balls, and then he tried to throw a curveball but it came inside rather than outside like some of the other pitches. I swung late again and caught it high enough on the handle of the bat to hit a home run to left field. So that was the end of the butterflies and I went around the bases giddy with happiness, never showing it of course, but there I was in the worse coordinated condition of my life, and I was two-for-two with a home run in the big leagues.

You had already made it to the big leagues and had played in games while with the Giants, so why were the "butterflies" still prevalent?

DT: Well, the butterflies were always caused by the fear of failure. That's one thing that I had a lot of in baseball because I don't think I ever had the roots of a real good confidence most kids had to have to be a good professional hitter. The only time that I was a good hitter was when I was feeling the bat in my hand and that comes about when you're in a good mental state and the physical strength in your hands is such that you have very good balance in your hands. Your hands are hitting as one. I wrote about that in my book because that's what the book is about. For me, those occurrences came few and far between. If only they had pitching machines in my time that I could get to. We never heard of anything like that where you could practice your swings. Usually by the midseason, my hands started feeling stronger but that's the way it went in baseball in those days.

Were you disappointed after your year in St. Louis to be selected in the expansion draft by the Houston Colt .45s? Would you have rather stayed with the Cardinals?

DT: Absolutely. When Dick Devine called me up and said, "Don, we just sold you to the Houston Colt .45s," I said, "Oh, no." I said, "I just loved it with you guys. You guys just made my whole life worth living." He said, "Well, you'll have a good chance to play regular now with them Don after the year you had with us." I said, "Yeah, after the year I had with you I

wanted to stay with you. I could make a nice contribution to your team next year too." He said the deal was done and "good luck" and that was it. So yes, I was disappointed. That year, unfortunately I tore my knee cartilage in the spring and that was the beginning of the end of my career. It was not a nice time.

In November of 1962 you were picked up by the Milwaukee Braves from the Colt .45s in the Minor League draft, but you never actually played for the Braves, right?

DT: No, I never played with the Braves. What happened was at the end of the 1962 season Paul Richards, with whom I had had a run-in, he was the Colt .45s general manager, and I don't like to talk about it because it's a very negative part of my career, but I had a run-in with him and he threatened me saying, "I'll see to it that you never play baseball in the big leagues again," and he did. That's another story though and I'd rather not get into that. They sold my contract to a "B" baseball club at the end of the season and Bobby Bragan, who was a coach with the Houston Colt .45s, became the manager with the Milwaukee Braves that next year and immediately picked up my contract and invited me to spring training with the Milwaukee Braves that year. Then, the next spring, they said they were sending me up to Toronto because they knew I had not played much the previous year. They were sending me to Toronto to get in shape and then they would bring me back up. I was two weeks into Toronto, and all of a sudden I got my release and that was the beginning of the end of my career. Paul Richards made his way into the other executive mansions of Major League Baseball.

When you were playing early on, whether in the minor leagues or in the majors, did it ever come to mind that at that time there were very few other Major League players that were in fact Jewish? Or, did you just see yourself as another ball player trying to make it and stay in the big leagues?

DT: Well, I knew there was a scarcity of Jewish ballplayers, sure. The Sherry brothers of the Dodgers I played against in the minor leagues because they were in my time and a couple of others, but I was never aware if I was playing against a Jewish player. We were just playing the game. I mean, we were kids and we could adjust to anything.

I guess what I'm getting at is, during that time I'm sure you witnessed what the black ballplayers had to go through. Did you ever experience anything similar?

DT: No, I was never afraid of it. Those guys really faced it because they couldn't hide their color. There was one story, a kid from the Bahamas. His father and mother came from a medical family, the father was a doctor. Andre Rogers of the New York Giants, later to be the San Francisco Giants, and he played with me on the Dallas team in the minors in the Texas League one year. Andre was six foot four and about two hundred and ten pounds. He was a good shortstop, a good prospect and one day during a time when the team was having a real great year in 1957, Andre came to me in the field, we were somewhere in Louisiana, Shreveport

I think, and he said, "Don, those guys behind our dugout are absolutely tormenting me. I can't concentrate on my game." I was considered kind of a leader because I was doing very well with the team. I told Andre I would try to take care of it. I took a bat out of the dugout and I asked two guys to follow me out. I said I was going to shut those guys up a few rows back behind our dugout because Andre was complaining about them taunting him. So I went over there and I said, "Look guys, let the ballplayers play, leave them alone. Stop taunting them." Meanwhile I was banging my bat against the pipe railing there separating them from us. I sort of banged the bat to let them know that if they don't shut up we were going to come and get them. That's the way it was in those days. You know, those guys get a few beers in them and they're yelling all kind of racist things at guys.

What was your mindset once you realized your baseball career was over?

DT: I was very bitter because it ended in a series of failures. I was still good enough to play ball, but I decided to change my lifestyle and try something else. But then, I think I tried one more year, somebody got in contact with me and said, "Would you like to play with us?" and I said, "Okay." Actually I went back to Dallas and played there, but nothing came of it and that was the end of it. Then I decided to continue on with something else and I went to work at Merrill Lynch, got married and had a family and left baseball behind. I had to support the family.

You've managed to keep baseball a part of your life for all of these years following your playing career.

DT: Well, the thing is, I think baseball has always been on my mind. After my business career, I got tired of that, I ended up buying a sports facility, a squash facility, and I owned it for twenty years in Mamaroneck, New York. During those twenty years I was a professional teaching pro there and I had to teach kids forehand and backhand strokes, and it was then that I learned about my failures because in teaching you learn a lot and I learned how to use my hands and I taught those kids how to use their hands. I said, "My goodness. I wish I had had this kind of an education during my baseball years." Twenty years of teaching thousands of kids how to hit with their hands. I also competed in squash a lot, I loved it. I was a very fast game. American squash is played with a hard rubber ball, a very fast game and I was very happy doing what I was doing. The only thing that stopped me from doing it was that the game changed and in order to keep up with the changes in the game, I had to change my courts to international and that would have required a big investment. The good lord stepped in and during a competitive game when I was sixty-six years old, I tore my Achilles tendon and that was the end of my competitiveness in squash and so I said, "Well, I might as well get out of the game," and I took everything I'd learned about the hands and try to help kids with baseball and teach them what I wish I had been taught years ago.

"Can you imagine that it's four in the morning and you're thirty thousand feet in a charter jet and you look over and there's Henry Aaron and Dusty Baker and Ralph Garr and there you are, a big league ball player? I don't know about some guys, but I loved that and I lived it every day."

NORMAN MILLER

Norm Miller

Norman Calvin Miller *was born in Los Angeles, California on February 5th of 1946 and says that he knew from a relatively early age that he was destined to become a Major League baseball player. His self-fulfilling prophecy ultimately became a reality when, after a very successful and impressive showing of his skills in high school, he was signed by the California Angels as an amateur free-agent in 1964 at the age of eighteen. As it turned out, he would never play for the Angels because he was then drafted by the Houston Colt .45s in the 1964 first-year draft. He would, however, go on to make his Major League debut at the age of nineteen with one at-bat against the Los Angeles Dodgers at Dodger Stadium on September 11, 1965 in which he recorded his first hit, a single off of Claude Osteen. He would go on to play in eleven games in late 1965 and then eleven more in 1966. Miller's career continued with the Colt .45s and the Astros until April of 1973, when he was traded to the Atlanta Braves. Little did he know at the time, but the three seasons he spent with the Astros between 1968 and 1970 would be the most productive of his career. With nagging back injuries slowing him down during his two seasons on Atlanta, he would play in only forty-five games before the Braves released him in October of 1974. One great memory that Miller carries with him from his brief time with the Braves was being in the dugout at old Atlanta-Fulton County Stadium the night Henry Aaron hit his 715th home run to break the all-time record held, of course, by Babe Ruth. It was a dugout view of one of the greatest highlights and moments in baseball history. He would then sign as a free-agent with the Dodgers in February of 1975 trying to make it as a utility player but was released by Los Angeles that April. Known for his defensive play during his 10 seasons, Miller finished with a career batting average of .238 with 24 home runs and 159 RBI's. He now lives in The Woodlands, near Houston. In 2009, he published a memoir* To All My Fans . . . From Norm Who?

Tell me a little bit about your early days as a kid growing up in Los Angeles and when it was that you first started to take an interest in sports and specifically in baseball.

NM: Well, I was born in 1946 in Los Angeles and in the 50's my family moved to the San Fernando Valley, which was just paradise. It was a block away from a Little League field, and I actually showed an interest in baseball when my father put a first baseman's glove in my crib when I came home from the hospital. There was no doubt from day one, whenever day one started, whether it was two or three or four years old that I was going to be a baseball player. I was totally one dimensional. From the moment I could get into an organized league, which was Little League at eight. By the time I was ten, I was fairly well known. I was arrogant and cocky and pretty good, and playing in Southern California, every day of my life was baseball, and that's all I ever wanted to be so I'm very fortunate that I did it.

Did you show enough promise and skill as a player early on to the point that you felt confident you would have a legitimate shot to make it to the majors?

NM: Yes, I think in Little League I was pretty highly talented. You know, when people talk about you at that age you get an idea that they're talking about something. And, you know, I loved the game. I just knew I was going to be a ball player, I made all the All-Star teams you're supposed to make, and I made all-league and all-world or whatever you're supposed to do. Actually, none of that really meant that much to me in the sense that it didn't surprise me. I really wasn't cocky; I guess people thought I was. I just really knew I was going to be a ball player. The only thing that I was afraid was that people were telling me I was too small. When I was a senior in high school, I remember the coach coming to me and saying, "The colleges are calling. What do you want me to tell them? How do you want to handle this?" Of course, back then everything was different than it is now, obviously, but I said "I'm not going to college. I'm going to be playing professional baseball." I don't think anybody else believed it. The scouts were interested, a lot of teams were interested but I was real small. I was a little second baseman, kind of the type of guy that when they were handing out uniforms they'd give them number one. But I signed and I'd decided that I would be in the big leagues in a couple of years and I was and that's just the way it was. I went to spring training with the same attitude, I'm going to be in the big leagues, the ball club kind of liked that attitude and ready or not I did not know any better so my whole life was just, I wanted to be a baseball player. Now my parents never said "You gotta go to college." My brother went on to be a lawyer and was a perfect student. I was a horrible student, always in trouble, the kind who liked to get in trouble. I was an adventuresome young man in Southern California but that's what the environment presented to me. I grew up on the beach having fun and then playing baseball and eating cheeseburgers so, you know, baseball from day one, I showed some ability that everyone took notice of and it worked out. There were a lot of kids back then that came out of Southern California and there still are.

Growing up, did your parents raise you in an observant Jewish home? What was their reaction when you made the decision to skip college and try and make baseball a career? Were they supportive of you and what you were trying to accomplish?

NM: Totally supportive. My brother was never told he should be a lawyer. Both my parents were raised in kosher houses but we weren't. My brother went through Hebrew school and was bar mitzvah'd, but I told my parents, "There ain't no way." When I made that statement at ten or eleven or whenever it was, whatever date you'd start Hebrew school, I told my parents that I wasn't going and they were not surprised because by then I had already established that I'm not doing anything you tell me. So, they told the rabbi and the rabbi's wife said, "Well, I'll give him private lessons," and unfortunately for her, when I went to her apartment to get my first private lesson it was overlooking the Little League field, so she did not stand a chance. After the first lesson I never went back. I was not raised with any of that. My dad was so thrilled that me and my brother played baseball, he was a pretty good ball player too but never had the desire, and my brother wanted to be a lawyer from day one. My parents were just thrilled that I could find anything to do to stay out of jail or to stay in school, so they were all for sports. They were great about that. My dad was a great teacher of the game and a pretty quiet guy so he was like my coach. He taught me everything. He played with us every day. I had an older brother to play catch with everyday.

In November of 1964, you're done with high school I assume, you sign with the California Angels as a free agent. Do you remember how excited you were at that time, to be that age, and be signing to play professional baseball?

NM: Well, there's a picture for a birthday or anniversary a few years ago, my wife had the picture of me that appeared in the local newspaper with my mom and dad with the scout signing me, a picture of me at eight years old in Little League and a picture of me in the big leagues. So, those three events were pretty cool and yeah, I remember it like it was yesterday. It was one of the most memorable days in my life. I had a very interesting thing happen in that when I was fifteen I was kind of discovered by the Angels before I was even discovered in high school. I mean, back then everything was free agency, scouts could sign anybody. I was invited to a Los Angeles Angels tryout camp because they had these big camps where they bring kids in, hundreds of kids, and it was a four-day camp. They cut kids everyday and this was the way they found kids. The reason it happened was my dad had gotten ill and was put in the hospital for over a year with tuberculosis, and a baseball coach of mine from a team I played on kind of became my surrogate father. He knew these scouts and he said, "Here's a kid whose dad is in the hospital, he's raising hell. Let him tryout, he's a good little ball player." So at fifteen I went to this tryout camp and I did real good the first day, and they invited me back the second day and the third day. On the fourth day I got to play, and I got four hits in the game and this was against all older kids. They took a liking to me, so then the next summer I got to work out, when the Angels and the Dodgers used to share Dodger Stadium, so the Angels invited me when I was sixteen, and I could drive to come to take batting practice every night with them and so for my junior year and senior year in high school in the summer, I went to Dodger Stadium every night and had my own locker, I was number 54. I took batting practice with Albie Pearson, Bob Perry, Jim Fregosi, and I took infield practice, so by the time I graduated, there was no doubt who I was going to sign with. There were probably five or six teams that were interested in me, but everybody knew I was going with the Angels. The only team that really came after me was Philadelphia. They spent a couple of days at my house trying to get me away from that thought, but I signed with the Angels. Can you imagine being fifteen or sixteen years old and you get to take infield practice with Leon Wagner and Bobby Knoop and Jim Fregosi? Pretty cool, huh?

You were actually drafted by the Houston Colt .45s from the Angels in the 1964 first-year draft. What happened with that?

NM: Well, I graduated high school in the summer of 1963. I signed at the end of the year. I don't know if you know the rules back then, but they still had this draft where you could draft Minor League players. Well, what happened was I signed with the Angels and went to Davenport, Iowa. I was having a really good year in the Midwest League. The scout that had signed me was in town watching me, and he told me that if I keep going, it was right after the All-Star break, that I was going to get moved up to Double-A or already Triple-A. Then I had a collision the next night at first base. I fell down and hurt my shoulder. I went to the hospital and was diagnosed with a mild separation which meant that I might be out a week or two. I went back to my apartment, and I got a call about midnight from the scout who had signed me. He was still at his hotel downtown at the Blackhawk Hotel, downtown Davenport. He told me to get in a cab and get to him, so I did. Now, it's one thirty in the morning. He has called my parents, who he knew obviously very well because he had scouted me for three years and had been to my home. He told my dad that I was coming home the next day and that I was through for the year. I was to go right to the Angels' office there in Hollywood and meet with the general manager, Fred Haney. So, we did that and they explained that they wanted to use this separated shoulder as a bogus way to hide me from the draft. They put in *The Sporting News* and all the papers that Norm Miller, prospect, sent home, career in doubt and in the meantime, the shoulder healed and they worked me out at a Little League field in Hollywood secretly for weeks. Then they had me come to the ball games, when the Angels were in town, with my arm in a sling so all the local scouts would see it. And so, we thought we had everybody fooled and I wouldn't be able to get drafted and they wouldn't lose me because they had signed Tom Egan from Los Angeles and Rick Reichert from Stevens Point for two hundred thousand dollars each. Back then that was enormous money, and they didn't want to lose those two guys and lose their money. They only could protect two players. I was the third and they had only given me twenty-five thousand dollars. So about a week before the draft, I got a call from a couple of teams. They said, "Hey, we want to know how your shoulder is." It wasn't considered tampering and I said, "Oh, God, I can't throw, my arm's shot," and they would hang up. Well, then a guy named Karl Kuehl called me. He went on to manage the Montreal Expos, and he was the scout for the Astros in that area, and he said, "We know there's nothing wrong because one of our scouts, Al Hollingsworth, was in Davenport the night you got hurt and he actually called the hospital and they said, 'No, it's was just a mild separation and he'll just be out a week or two.'" So the whole thing was they knew and they had the first draft pick the next day and they took me off the roster, so that's how I became an Astro.

You went on to make your Major League debut in September of 1965 in a game against the Dodgers. That's got to go down as one of the most exciting days in your life, I'm sure.

NM: Oh, without a doubt. I had gotten called up and I drove from Tulsa, Oklahoma where they told me I was playing in Double-A and the manager called me in and said, "You're going to join the team next Tuesday so when we go back tonight pack your car." So I drove from Amarillo non-stop to LA. I ran off the road in Barstow when I fell asleep. Got home and rested for a while. A couple of days later I drove up to Dodger Stadium and walked into the clubhouse and it was, without a doubt, like they always say, "Well, except for the birth of my children. Bullshit." This was it! Luman Harris was the manager and he called me in and said, "I don't like rookies. Glad you had a good year, so go out there and let all the fans and your family see you. I know this is your home, and then when the game starts sit as far away from me as possible." I did that and then in the eighth inning Claude Osteen was pitching and it was a close game and then someone yelled "Miller, get a bat!" and they meant me! I didn't know that because he had said that I wasn't going to play and it's a left-handed pitcher and I'm left-handed so on the second "Miller, get a bat," I looked and they were calling me. I stumbled out of the dugout and walked up to home plate and the umpire looked at me and said, "Son, it's a lot easier to hit in the big leagues if you take your jacket off." I stepped in to home plate petrified, strike one, strike two, and then I stepped out and Osteen, who had great control, threw two balls so it was 2-2 and to this day, I can remember taking a deep breath and I made up my mind that the moment his arm gets above his head I'm swinging. And I swung and I hit a line drive right up the middle. I stood at home plate and Willie Davis almost threw me out at first base because I was in shock. I could hear my mom screaming in the stands. It was my hometown. A year earlier I was sneaking out of school to go sit in the bleachers and watch these guys play. So, I got to first base and they gave me the ball and then I introduced myself to Wes Parker and shook his hand and then I stole second and slid into Maury Wills, called timeout and shook his hand because I just thought I may never be around here again. I just had a great time.

You played in eleven games in 1965. Was it a situation where you were a September call-up?

NM: I came up from the minors at the end of the year. I had a real good year at Double-A so they brought me up and that's when I got my first hit. I played the last two or three weeks, played in a couple games with them and had a ball. I mean, just being in the big leagues for two or three weeks was just incredible. I was starting my first game in Pittsburgh and got to run out and stand in the footprints of Roberto Clemente. I mean it doesn't get any better than that. I stood in his footprints.

You played in eleven games again in 1966. Where were you assigned to in the minor leagues?

NM: Oklahoma City. I went to Triple-A when I was nineteen. I started in A-ball with the Angels, then I got drafted and went to Double-A and had a good year then I went to Triple-A, and that was in 1966. I did okay, not bad. They were happy. In 1967 I came up and down a couple of times. One of the problems we had back then is I was in the Army reserves because of the Vietnam War, and I had to join the Army and I was in the reserves so I was going to Army meetings for two years all the time. I'd be in Oklahoma City, and I'd play a game on a Friday night and they'd fly me down, all night down to Houston and I'd go to reserve meetings for the weekend. So, for about two years I never got to play a lot. I mean, almost every weekend, or every two weeks, I had to fly to Houston for Army meetings and that continued when I was in the big leagues too.

In 1969 you broke through and played in 119 games, getting 409 at-bats, and that was the year you played in the most number of games.

NM: In 1969 I finally got my shot. I'm twenty-two years old and I'm doing great. I was hitting between .290 and .300 all year. I'm playing for a guy named Harry Walker and for some reason, after playing in a hundred and something straight games, I sit out a game in San Diego and then I sit out another game in San Diego and then I sit out a doubleheader, and back then they didn't tell you shit. Then we go to Pittsburgh and I'm pissed off because all the players are on my ass for not playing, you know, players didn't like that back then. I didn't know why I wasn't playing. I just played hard and I was having a great year hitting cleanup and I'm not even a cleanup hitter. I was listed in one sports magazine as one of the ten most underrated players in the big leagues by Walter Alston and Maury Wills. You know, I was just doing what they expected out of me, and then I don't play three days and then we go into Pittsburgh and I'm not in the lineups and I'm pissed off. In the ninth inning, I just figured the pitcher's leading off, it's a close ballgame, Bob Moose is pitching, a right-hander, so I just went down between innings and put on my helmet and got my bat and figured I'm going to lead off the inning pinch-hitting. I got half way to the plate and Harry Walker called me back. He said, "You're not hitting." So I threw my helmet at him and my bat and I left the ballpark. The next morning, he and I got into a big argument and I basically hit him. So that was it. I stayed with that organization for several more years because back then free agency wasn't free agency, and when I finally got traded, I got traded to the Braves, but I had a spine injury. So that's my career. You know, that's what baseball did. You couldn't move around. I can tell you that at the end of the 1969 season, I walked into the general manager's office, because the rest of the year I didn't play. I mean, I did everything you can to get traded. I made no bones about it. Harry Walker was a racist and he was a prick, and the general manager, Spec Richardson, was a drunk and I wasn't going to stay there. You know, I'd never taken much crap in my life. I'm not saying it's right or wrong, and the day the season was over I went in the general manager's office. I walked right through Ann Wallace, his secretary, and Spec Richardson's on the phone and he turns around and he says, "Five teams want you already but you're not going anywhere so get the hell out of here." That's how they talked to you back then. They kept me for the next five years, and Harry Walker stayed as manager, so what are you going to do?

Well let me ask you then, since you used the word "racist." Do you think you were treated like you were because you were a Jewish player?

NM: Well, let me answer it this way because I have to be real careful here. You know, life went on and life's been good. Okay. I don't know. I know that years later, and I mean years later, I was told something by someone from the organization, a guy who was fairly high up in our organization. He's not alive anymore. He must have had guilt or something because it was probably twenty years later at a ball game in the Astrodome, he came up to me, and this was a guy who wasn't even my friend in the front office. This was a guy who had no reason to do this but made a statement that kind of referred to the fact that yeah, yeah, and that's what other people said. I have never said it because I have no proof but Harry Walker, from Leeds, Alabama? You know, if he was alive today I'd kill him again. He was not liked and he was not revered. You know, when a when a guy comes up to me one day, a manager comes up to me and says, "Hey, I want you to meet a friend of mine, he's Jewish," I don't buy into that too much and you being one you understand. There was no reason, and I'm sixty-three years old, I'm having a great life so I'm not a bitter person. I'm a pretty happy-go-lucky guy. I had a great time playing in the big leagues. If my back had not gone out I would have had five or six more good years playing right field for the Braves. That's why they traded for me. It didn't work out but I got ten years in the big leagues and I hit a home run, I hit a grand slam. I did it all. Did it turn out the way I wanted?

No, but it was still great. I don't live for yesterday but I could play. I proved I could play. You don't stay in the big leagues for ten years and then get traded for someone unless you can play. But the organization wouldn't let me go. They'd made a bad trade with Joe Morgan through the Cincinnati Reds. They weren't going to make another trade of any young ball players and there I sat. I was a good pinch-hitter, I had the respect of my friends, the players liked me, the fans liked me because they've been great to me here in this town for thirty-five years. So, you know, in the end I look back, shit, what are you going to say? But between you and me, you're damn right I think there was something there, damn right.

You did not play in too many games while in Atlanta, but you certainly were fortunate to be a Brave when you were.

NM: Absolutely. Let me tell you something—every day was historical. You've got to understand, you know, I'm kind of this impressionable guy in the sense that I really get up every day to have a good time and I'm more of a creative person, I've been in the creative world all of my life. So, I look at the world visually. Can you imagine that it's four in the morning and you're thirty thousand feet in a charter jet and you look over and there's Henry Aaron and Dusty Baker and Ralph Garr and there you are, a big league ball player? I don't know about some guys, but I loved that and I lived it every day. I mean, I loved it after I struck out. You know, I'd be pissed off but then I'd say, "I'm in the big leagues!" When I hear ball players today call themselves entertainers, I just laugh. They don't get it. They say they're not role models. Back when I was a kid being a role model was an honor. If you could become a role model, wow, you've made it. You know, you're family would be proud of you and I still look at it that way. I have conversations every day about baseball. A guy says, "You played. You hustled." I mean, what else can you ask for? Would I have liked to have had a better chance? Absolutely. I could have been a good ball player, I mean I could have been a guy who hit .270, .280, hit maybe 10, 12 home runs and drive in 80 runs and not make any errors and that's pretty good. We're not all going to be Mays, Clemente, and Aaron. Right now there are some guys in the big leagues who could not have made the big leagues when I played because the talent pool is not what it once was. But, they're making eighteen million dollars a year, more power to them. I think it's absolutely great that this thing is so screwed up.

Were you in the dugout the night Hank Aaron hit his 715th home run at Atlanta-Fulton County Stadium?

NM: I was right there and I lockered next to him.

Talk about what it was like in the stadium that night.

NM: Well, Henry was a great guy. Henry was a jokester. He got a bad rap. He was a great guy. It was history and we couldn't wait. The players loved him and anybody that played with Henry, sure you respected him, idolized him, and all of us back then were from a different era. We worshipped these guys. We had these guys' baseball cards. It was a great thrill. We were so relieved for Henry. We were so empathetic for what he was going through, the death threats and such. He never talked about it, but we knew what he was going through. So, it was one of those evenings where how many people were fortunate to be on the bench, you know? Another great thrill was a comical thing. When he announced he was going to Milwaukee to end his career the next year, of course the last night of his last game in the National League, Fulton County Stadium was full and the fans wanted him to hit a home run. I think the first time up he went up and squared up like he was going to bunt and they probably booed him because that's the way it was back then. And then right before he went up to hit the second time, I was standing by the bat rack and of course my career was already through. I was in uniform but I didn't even wear a jock. I mean, I hadn't played in a year and a half. The doctors already said I was through and I was just waiting to finish this last game, get in my car and drive home. Again, Henry was at the bat rack and he said, "This will be my last home run I ever hit in the National League." That's what he said to me. So Henry went up and he hit a home run and back then they didn't have curtain calls, but in this case they were demanding one, and Henry never came out. In fact, Henry was already up in the locker room. He literally left the field and went in the locker room. I ran up the tunnel. I go in there and Henry is already out of his uniform and in his slacks and he basically said, "I'm leaving." I mean, at the end of his career in Atlanta, I don't think it was a real good relationship with the organization. And Henry just was leaving and he handed me his shoes and he said, "Here, here's my shoes." So I had the last pair of Henry Aaron's shoes that he ever hit a National League home run in. I kept them for something like thirty years. I wrapped them in plastic and stuck them in a closet because memorabilia was nothing back then and hell, we didn't keep anything. So, a number of years ago I was cleaning out my closet and I came across the shoes, the mud still in the cleats although it was dry dirt, sealed in plastic. I went to the ball park, I was working in the front office for the Astros, and Larry Dierker was the announcer then, this was prior to him being the manager, and the team was getting ready to go on a road trip to Atlanta. I gave Larry the shoes and said, "Hey, take these back to Henry and give them to him." He called me, and he remembered and thought it was great. Most people thought I should have sold them. I'm not selling shoes. First of all, what am I going to do, call Henry and say, "Hey, I need some money. Can you send me a letter of authenticity?" But that was a great thrill. I mean, that was what was so cool about baseball. You know, I play golf three or four days a week with an ex-ball player, a guy who caught in the big leagues for fifteen years, made the All-Star team, John Edwards. He seventy years old and we sit around and drink beer and every once in a while tell a story of some guys. I love it, I just love it.

In 1967, while you were with the Astros, interestingly enough you were one of four Jewish players on the roster with Larry Sherry, Barry Latman, and Bo Belinski. Was that ever a topic of conversation for you guys, the fact that there were four of you who were Jewish on the same club?

NM: Probably, but it's just like saying there were four black guys. That was the interesting thing. You know, I've had ball players call me say, "Shut up you rotten Jew" and it never in my wildest dreams bothered me. We were so close back then that we could do that and it wouldn't be out of disrespect. I'm sure one time Latman or me or someone made a remark, "You guys want to go to temple with us," or something and guys would laugh. I literally never saw anything disrespectful. I mean sometimes we'd hear someone say "Hey Jew, you playing tonight?" You know, who cares. I didn't bother me. It was nothing to me. We poked fun at ourselves. You couldn't do it today, but we sure did back then.

Who was the toughest pitcher you faced?

NM: Bob Gibson. I never had to face Koufax. If I had faced Koufax I would have said Koufax, but he was in a league totally on his own. Then there was Gibson and I think most guys will say Gibson and Koufax. Gibson was a competitor, I mean nobody even comes close other than maybe Tom Seaver and Koufax. Gibson had overpowering stuff. He had two pitches, fastball and breaking ball, both of them overpowering. He was intimidating, he had tremendous control and I never got a hit against Bob Gibson. I played every game against him because nobody else wanted to. We had guys who knew what night Gibson was pitching and they'd "get sick" the day before. We used to call it "Gibsonitis." Then finally right at the end of my career I hit a ground ball to shortstop, Dal Maxvill, and he threw me out. But I was so happy that I had hit the ball that when I was running across the field towards the dugout, I yelled to Gibson, "I got ya," and it's a good thing I never faced him again because he would have hit me again.

You signed as a free agent with the Dodgers in February of 1975 and then you were released that April. At that point, what was it like to realize that your dream was coming to an end?

NM: What had happened was, if you go back to 1973, the first week in the season, Leo Durocher was our manager. I was with the Astros, and I was getting ready to go to the ballpark with Tommy Helms and Jimmy Stewart, we're waiting on a cab in front of the Biltmore Hotel in LA I opened the door to get in the cab and I had a pain in my back that literally knocked me down. I thought I'd been shot by a bullet. So Helms and Stewart, being the compassionate bastards that ball players are, just picked me up and threw me in the cab. I had thought I'd been shot. We got to Dodger Stadium, it was a short drive, and they left me there. So the cabbie went in the clubhouse and they came out and had to get a wheel chair. I was in the most pain I'd ever had in my life and this was around four o'clock in the afternoon. I'm laying on the training table just in agony and they're trying to get a hold of the Dodgers' doctor, Dr. Kurland. Durocher comes in and stands over me and just yells, "What the hell happened to him?" He was pissed. Well, it turns out he was pissed because he was waiting for me to come in to tell me that I had just been traded to the Braves, which was on a Tuesday. So they didn't tell me I was traded. They strapped me in a jet and flew me to Houston. I got in early in the morning, and my wife picked me up and took me to the orthopedic surgeon, Dr. Brosword, and he examined it and said it was a severe strain and muscle spasms. I knew it was not a severe strain. They wanted to put me in the hospital, and I said no so they sent me home and sedated me, basically to relax the muscles. On Saturday the general manager called me and said, "Can you come to the ball park?" That was crazy Spec Richardson. My wife loaded me in the car and we went, but I could hardly walk. I was in agony. I spent the evening in his box watching the game with my wife. We came home, walked in the door about eleven o'clock at night, the phone rang and it was the general manager Spec, who I'd just left, and he said, "Norm," and I'd been with the organization about nine years, he said, "We just traded you to the Braves. Good luck" and hung up. The phone rang a minute later and it was Eddie Robinson, the general manager of the Braves and Eddie Matthews, who was the manager and my former roommate in 1967. They said, "Hey, we've been trying to get you for two years. You're starting in right field and I'm moving Aaron in to first base." I knew these guys because Eddie Robinson, to show you the irony, Eddie Robinson was the farm director for the Astros who's gotten me away from the Angels. So here's the farm director who knew me and here's my ex-roommate from '67 Eddie Matthews and my boyhood idol. I thought that was kind of neat but I said, "Don't make the trade," and they said, "We know all about your back, we made the trade Tuesday but we've been waiting for the doctors' reports and our doctors have talked to your doctors and we know it's a muscle spasm." I said, "No, it's not a muscle spasm guys, I'm telling you." So, they said, and this was on Saturday night, they said, "Join us Tuesday in Atlanta," and Eddie Robinson said, "I'll pick you up at the airport," and I got off in a wheel chair and went right to Piedmont Hospital and that was it. They sent me to Illinois eventually to have an experimental procedure done on my spine. I came back and played one game, but it didn't work. I came back for spring training the next year and the back didn't hold up. I asked to be released during the middle of '74. In fact, I asked Eddie Robinson, "Hey, I'm through. Let me go home and start my other career." They made me stay the whole year, the pricks. Then I went home and what happened was, I had a good job waiting for me, and in January I got a call from the Dodgers, from Al Campanis. If you go back in history, the Dodgers used to love to sign veteran left-handed hitters to pinch-hit. They used to always get these guys who'd been around and Walter Alston had always been a fan of mine, you know, he had voted me as one of the ten most underrated players in baseball one time. Campanis said, "Look it, we know you've had back problems and we know you're an LA guy," and my home was in Houston then, and he said, "Would you have any interest in joining the Dodgers just to pinch-hit and be an extra outfielder? We know you can catch because we've seen you catch in batting practice." And I said, "Well," and by then my back had been rested, "Well, just to pinch-hit, I don't know." The next day they flew me out for a physical. I flew out to LA, I took a cab to Dr. Kurland's office, they examined me thoroughly, and I went back to the airport and flew home. Dr. Kurland said to the Dodgers, "I think he can hold up. If he doesn't have to play a lot I think his back can hold up." I signed and they asked me to come out to LA in the month of February and work out with the team in Dodger Stadium prior to going to spring training, which we did. My wife and I were really excited about this, getting to play for my hometown team. I went to spring training and things fell apart and I knew my career was over then for sure because the fifth week of spring training, and keep in mind that I only had been up to the plate eleven times in two years in the big leagues, and I was struggling in spring training. I was missing the pitches I used to hit, and we were playing in Daytona Beach, an exhibition game near the end of spring training, and I hit a ground ball to the shortstop and they threw me out by two feet and I knew that, one, I had lost my quick bat, I was missing a lot of fastballs, and two, I had lost my speed. It was just a matter of time. There was a cut to be made the last day and I was the guy they cut. All in all I've never looked back. I had a job waiting for me and I never looked back.

What kind of a job did you have waiting for you? What kind of work did you get into?

NM: I basically became a marketing and advertising person and I've had real good success at it. I had a talent and I didn't know it. I worked every off-season in Houston because I didn't make enough money to live year round. I'd always work because I knew the career would come to an end and in that period of being a ball player and well known in Houston I met a couple of guys who owned a large company, a chain of restaurants, so I had my real estate license so they hired me to do site locations for their chain. When I left them we had ninety of them around three states. When I joined them they had around forty. I started out as the director of real estate and a year later I showed an aptitude for advertising, kind of the creative route, so I took over the advertising and stayed with them for a number of years and then just continued from then on. You know, I'm still in it. I was the vice-president of marketing for a large Texas bank for a number of years, and then eight years ago I left the bank and they kept me on the payroll as a paid consultant and I'm still on the payroll.

When you look back on your baseball career, being that you were a Jewish ball player and part of such a small minority group within the game itself, is it something that you're still proud of these many years later?

NM: On a scale of one to ten about a twenty. Absolutely, I mean, who wouldn't want to be? Look at what I got to do, look at what I got to experience, look at the doors it opened. Fortunately I was smart enough to realize it opened doors. The other thing I realized as a young man is that it does open doors to give you an advantage only if you had a brain or if you knew how to do something. To this day people say to me, "What do you do, play golf with customers of the bank?" Once you're an athlete you have no brain, but I've gone on and I realized years ago it doesn't matter. The only thing that matters is that whoever's paying you is getting the results and that's it. Then sooner or later people will take notice, and I've gotten a ton of publicity and I've gotten my due in business too. But, you know what? I never talk about my business. Who wants to talk about business? What do they want to hear to this day? Baseball. "What was it like when you played?" "Tell me a story. What was Doug Rader like?" "Did you ever know Henry Aaron?" How many people get to be able to carry on a conversation about that? I've made a living doing it. I was on the radio for a number of years, why? Because I was Norm Miller the ball player. I do public speaking. Why? Because I talk about teamwork. Well, where did you learn team work? Because I know what teamwork really is. I know what a good team is and I know what makes a bad team, and it's not all the bullshit that people talk about, so I go out and people pay me to go speak about it. Well, it's because I was a ball player and I worked hard and I made it and I did it. I hit a grand slam once. I struck out with the bases loaded. I made a beautiful catch one time and another time I dropped a fly ball in front of fifty-thousand people at Dodger Stadium. I stole a base and got picked off. I did it all, you know? I sat down and talked to Roberto Clemente during a rain delay. Come on, it doesn't get any better than that to talk to your boyhood idol. I'm proud that I made it to the big leagues and I'm proud that I stayed. I'm proud that when it was all over with people remembered that I hustled. Then, the thing it taught me was that, you know, when I got into the business was "You don't know shit. Just do what you did in baseball. Outwork everybody and have a pretty good attitude and try to have fun." It's been my life.

"The only time religion came up into it was in the World Series in 1959 when I decided that I wasn't going to pitch on Yom Kippur, and then Koufax and Sherry agreed. Of course, now it's all about Koufax, but that's fine. We decided that, and we didn't pitch."

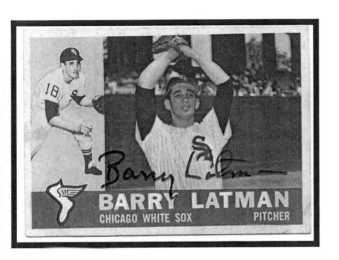

BARRY LATMAN

Arnold Barry Latman *was born in Los Angeles in May of 1936. While growing up in an observant Jewish home, he took an interest in playing baseball at the age of eight. After playing for a couple of years, he had to take time away from the game in order to begin practicing for his bar mitzvah. At thirteen he began to play again and did so through high school, where in 1954 he was voted to participate in an all-star game in New York City. At that point he was offered a bonus to sign a professional contract. His parents and grandfather, though, had other ideas for him. Barry declined and instead signed a baseball scholarship to attend the University of Southern California. As it would turn out, he was not a Trojan for long. In 1955, Latman signed his first Major League contract with the Chicago White Sox and began his pro career in the minors in Waterloo, Iowa. That first season in Iowa he went 18-5 with an ERA of 4.12. Not a bad season for the Jewish kid from California. After stops in Memphis and Indianapolis in 1956 and 1957, Latman made his Major League debut with the White Sox on September 10, 1957 as a late season call-up. He would enjoy his first career victory five days later with a win over the Washington Senators at Griffith Stadium. In 1958 he split the season between Indianapolis and Chicago. In 1959, while going 8-5 with an ERA of 3.78 in 156 innings pitched, the White Sox won the pennant and advanced to the World Series where they lost to the Dodgers four games to two. Unfortunately, Latman did not get a chance to pitch in the series. The Dodgers, meanwhile, had a Jewish hurler of their own, Larry Sherry, Norm's brother, who won two games and was named the series MVP. In April of 1960, the White Sox traded Latman to the Cleveland Indians for Herb Score. He spent four seasons in Cleveland, his best being 1961 when he went 13-5 in 45 appearances. That year he was selected for the American League All-Star team, but like the World Series two years earlier, did not get a chance to pitch. The game ended early in a 1-1 tie due to rain. In December of 1963 he was traded to the Los Angeles Angels where he won seven games over two seasons before being traded to the Houston Astros in December of 1965. By this time he was no longer starting but was pitching in relief. He went on to win five games in ten starts during the1966 and 1967 seasons before the Astros released him in August of 1967. In* *his eleven year Major League career, Latman posted a record of 59-68 in 344 games with 134 starts with an ERA of 3.91. Also throughout his career, he had 332 at-bats in which he managed 48 hits with 2 home runs and 25 RBI's. Barry now lives in Puerto Vallarta, Mexico.*

How much do you remember of your early years growing up and learning the game of baseball?

BL: Well, I started, of course, in Los Angeles. I lived there all my life. My father was a baseball player in Brooklyn, but in those days they didn't have professional teams so much. They had the major leagues, but they did not have any minor leagues, and he played semi-pro baseball. We started playing Cub Scout baseball when I was eight years old. By the time I turned ten I had to quit to become bar mitzvah'd. My grandfather was living in the house, so my father promised me that after I was bar mitzvah'd, if he had to, he would sponsor a team, and I would be able to start playing baseball again. And that's what happened. So for three years there was no baseball and a lot of studying. And then, when I became bar mitzvah'd, my father kept his word, and we started playing baseball again. We played in a traveling league, which was out of Los Angeles. They didn't have any little leagues in those days, but they did have a traveling league with guys in high school. I was thirteen, and I got to join them. I started playing baseball then, and I continued all the way through school and through high school. I was voted while in high school to represent California in an All-Star game in New York City. From there I went to USC for a year and decided that I wanted to go into professional baseball, and I signed with the White Sox and that's basically the way it started.

One of your baseball highlights while in high school was pitching a perfect game. Tell me about that game.

BL: The perfect game I pitched, all the scouts were there. That was the day they were scouting me. I pitched twenty-one straight outs and I struck out nineteen.

What was it like for you to be traveling across the country to play in that all-star game in New York? Was that the first time for you on an airplane?

BL: It was the first time I'd ever flown in an airplane, and we flew for ten and a half hours. In those days you were facing backwards. It wasn't on a jet of course. I got to play in the Polo Grounds and Ebbets Field and Yankee Stadium that time so it was a great thrill. At that point I was absolutely ready to play professional. I wanted to play professional, but my grandfather and father said, "No, you have to go to college." So I went to college for a year and finally talked them in to letting me play.

You mentioned that scouts had come to see you while you were in high school. What team offered you that first contract?

BL: In those days they had bonus rules. If you got a six thousand dollar bonus or more, you'd have to play in the major leagues for two years, so I had all the teams come. I had Branch Rickey in my house, and I had quite a few of them from all over, including Charles Comiskey and the White Sox. I even had the Yankees there, so we got to meet a lot of people. Of course there were only eight teams in each league at that time. Branch Rickey offered me the opportunity to start out at the Hollywood ballpark, which was about three blocks away from my house. My mother wanted me to, but my father and I decided against it.

In the end the decision was made that you were not going to sign a professional contract right out of high school. You were going to go to college. Whose decision was that?

BL: That was my parents' decision, for me to go to college. I would have signed right out of high school.

So you went to the University of Southern California. What happened while you were there?

BL: Actually, I got to leave Southern Cal because they wanted to change my style of pitching. Rod Dedeaux wanted to make me come over, up higher, and I was just throwing pretty good at that time. I didn't want to change. My father said "No, no, no." So when Dedeaux came over and said, "I think we should change you, bring his arm up a little bit," my father said, "No, I think we'll let him sign professionally." So that's what happened.

In 1954 you began corresponding with Ty Cobb. How did that come about?

BL: When I was my second year in high school, I had some honors, and my head was getting kind of big. My father had a friend who knew Ty Cobb. He said to me, "Let's go talk to Ty Cobb," and I said "Oh, of course, ah ha." We actually went up to San Francisco. He was living in Palo Alto at the time, and I spent a whole afternoon with him. We talked and talked about how tough it would be to play professional baseball, how you think you're great, and when you go out there, every one of those players you're playing with thinks they're great, so you better not think you're too good because you have to prove it every day. We started corresponding, and I have his letters, about six or seven I guess, from every year until he passed away.

TYRUS R. COBB
GLENBROOK
DOUGLAS COUNTY, NEVADA 9/2/54

Dear Barry:- your letter received a
few days ago, I appreciate your
writing me.
I have read in papers about you
and your accomplishments:
May I wish you every success
and might I say, you yourself
must make good, no one else
can help you, so go out there
with your head on your shoulders
and think you are master, no
one else can help you, I will have
to say, get all you can, but start
low in your class and develop,
Much luck,   Sincerely
                      Ty Cobb

Ty Cobb letter to Barry Latman in September 1954

Interestingly, though, Ty Cobb was well often thought to be an anti-Semite and a racist.

BL: I don't believe that. All I can tell you is that he knew that we were Jewish. He came to my house in Los Angeles and to Gilmore Field. Every time he would go to LA, he would call me up and invite me to come to these different banquets, and I'd be his guest, and I had no problems. I never felt that, but of course, in baseball you can get reputations that really aren't truthful.

So you saw another side of Ty Cobb.

BL: Absolutely, and these letters that I have, if you would read them, you would see another complete side. You see a man that took an interest and really tried to help me. The amazing thing is every time he would see me on television he would write me a letter. When I say "saw me pitch on television he'd write a letter," that is because in those days they only had one game of the week on Saturdays. It was the only baseball game televised at that point, and most of them were in New York. But I did pitch in a couple of them, and I'd get a letter from Ty Cobb saying, "I saw you pitch and do this and do that." He was only out to help me; he was not out to hurt me at all.

You signed with the White Sox after that first year in college. It must have been very exciting for you to sign that first professional contract.

BL: It was a great thrill. I went down to spring training with the White Sox in Sarasota, and the story that I tell now is that when I arrived, there were six other guys that flew in that morning and we all went to the ballpark. They picked us up at the airport and said, "Come bring your stuff and go to the ball park." They worked us out, and we did not know that four of the six were being sent back that afternoon. They only had room for two players. I was lucky enough to be one of the two that stayed. The rest of them went back that same night and, of course, we signed the six thousand dollar bonus which wasn't too much.

You get assigned to the White Sox Minor League team in Waterloo, Iowa in 1955. What was that like for you, going from living in California to Iowa on your first professional baseball assignment?

BL: Well, being the first time you're away from home, it wasn't bad at all. We'd have these long road trips and it was a lot of fun, you know, and I was just a young kid. I lived in a house, a boarding house and the lady would let me sleep on the porch because there was no air conditioning in those days. When you're young you can do those things. I don't think I could do it right now, and I don't think I would want to go back and do it, but we would ride a bus all night long. But the biggest thing was if you were the starting pitcher, the next day you got a whole seat to yourself.

You had a pretty good year there in 1955. You won 18 ball games.

BL: Yeah, I got lucky. I had a lot of support and that's all it is. If you get the runs when you pitch, you do pretty well.

In 1956 you were promoted to Memphis in the Southern Association and then to Indianapolis. It was then in September of 1957 that you got your first call up to the major leagues. Do you remember walking into that clubhouse for the first time and then pitching in your first game?

BL: Yes, that was kind of exciting. I was a scared little boy. It was amazing. Dick Donovan and Early Wynn came over and said, "Don't worry about it son, everybody has the same feeling."

And five days later, you won your first game pitching against the Washington Senators.

BL: You have to be lucky to a point when you get your chance. You've got to be able to perform. That's the difference between guys that stay in the minor leagues for eight or nine or ten years and guys that come right up. When they do get their break, no matter how they get it, they do perform.

It was in 1959 that you finally made the majors for good with the White Sox. Looking back, you really only spent two to three seasons in the minor leagues.

BL: Actually, the problem was that in 1959 my father passed away. We had to sit shiva, and I missed ten or twelve days of spring training. That was a very tough season, even though it was the first season, because I would normally call home after every game, and my father and my mother and I would get on the phone, and my father and I would talk over every game. It was like I had lost my best coach.

I'm sure your mother and father were very proud of you to have made the major leagues.

BL: Yes, but you have to hear the funny story. When I quit USC my grandfather disowned me. He wouldn't talk to me at all because he had come over from the old country. He'd said I was going to be the first one in the family to have a college education, and I quit after the first year. Finally, I think in 1958, I pitched in Yankee Stadium one day on television. He saw that, and he called me up in the clubhouse, and he let me come back in the family. No one could get through to the clubhouse in those days, but my grandfather got through.

In 1959 you were still in Chicago and you went 8-5, and the next thing you know the White Sox advance to the World Series. Unfortunately, you did not get to pitch in the series.

BL: I was supposed to pitch the fourth game but our manager, Al Lopez, comes up to me and says, "Well, we've lost two, and if I lose with you tomorrow it's over with, but if I lose with Early Wynn nothing will happen," so that's what happened, I lost my start.

Larry Sherry was pitching with the Dodgers and was the MVP of that series in 1959. Did you know him and his brother Norm?

BL: I went to high school with Larry Sherry. Sherry and I were best of friends. Norm's his brother. He was older than us. We played high school ball together.

Was there ever any talk between you guys that there really were not a lot of Jewish players in the major leagues, and how special it was for you to be there and be playing?

BL: No, religion wasn't brought into it at all. The only time religion came up into it was in the World Series in 1959 when I decided that I wasn't going to pitch on Yom Kippur, and then Koufax and Sherry agreed. Of course, now it's all about Koufax, but that's fine. We decided that, and we didn't pitch.

In 1960 you were traded to the Cleveland Indians. You had your best season while with them in 1961, going 13-5 and earning a spot on the American League All-Star team.

BL: I had a contract for that year that if I won over ten games, I think I got paid a thousand dollars a win after that. I won the eleventh game and then they took me out of the rotation and put me in the bullpen because they were losing by that time, and they didn't want to pay me. So I got a couple of more thousand, but that was about it. It was a super season. You get lucky. You know, I pitched as good the next year, but I didn't win, so figure it out.

You made the All-Star team, but it had to be disappointing to not get a chance to actually pitch in the game.

BL: Well, what happened was that was the only All-Star game that's been rained out, and I was going to be pitching the next inning.

You left Cleveland following the 1963 season and went back out to the West Coast with the Los Angeles and then California Angels. You spent your last two seasons with the Houston Astros. Could you sense that your career was winding down at that point?

BL: Well, at that point they started putting me in the bullpen, so I knew it was ending because in those days, once you get to the bullpen, it was only a matter of time. That's what happened. Now it's a different game completely. In those days you stayed in the bullpen for a couple of years and that's it.

Who would you say some of the greatest players were that you played with?

BL: Well, I played with a lot of Hall of Famers, guys like Luis Aparicio and Nellie Fox. I played with Ted Kluszewski. Early Wynn is probably the best pitcher I saw, and he was just winding his career down. I played with Robin Roberts one year.

From a pitcher's standpoint, who were the toughest hitters you faced?

BL: Well, the first hitter I ever faced in the major leagues was a pretty good hitter, Ted Williams. He walked. The next day we took a train to New York, and then I faced a guy by the name of Mickey Mantle my next game there. They broke me in pretty good against some pretty good hitters. The toughest hitter I ever had to face was Joe DeMaestri. I think I faced him ten times, and he got nine hits and I hit him once. I know I never got him out.

When it was all said and done you appeared in 344 games. When you look back at it, was it one of the best times of your life, to be that young and playing professional baseball?

BL: It was the greatest time in my whole life. I'm seventy-two years old right now, and I can reflect back on it, and it was absolutely the best time in my whole life. You know, it's something that you grow up wanting to do, you know you can do it. Then you prove that you can play there, and that's the hardest thing because there's nobody that's going to go out there and throw the ball for you, and there's nobody that's going to hit the ball for you. So, that's the best part about it.

*"I played against some of the best—Stan Musial, Ted Williams. . . .
I played against the Dodgers when they had some pretty fair
ball players. I played in a great era."*

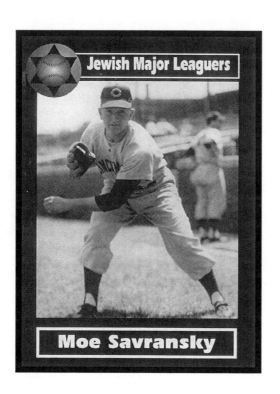

MORRIS SAVRANSKY

Morris Savransky

There's no question *that if* **Morris Savransky** *had pitched during the modern era of baseball, with today's sports medicine advancements, he could have played in more than just the sixteen games that he appeared in with the 1954 Cincinnati Reds. As he tells it, it was the wear and tear of throwing the screwball that caused the arm problems that ended his career prematurely. Savransky was born in Cleveland, Ohio on January 13, 1929 and was a prospect by the time he reached Cleveland Heights High School. After pitching in the Ohio State High School Championships and leading his team to the state title, as well as the Amateur World Series in 1947, Savransky went to Ohio State University on a basketball scholarship. As it turned out he wasn't a Buckeye athlete for long. Although he would continue his college education in the off-season, in 1948 Savransky signed an amateur free agent contract with the Cincinnati Reds and was assigned to their Class-B team in Sunbury, Pennsylvania. He finished 6-4 with a 3.67 ERA that first year as a professional. He spent 1949 in Charleston, West Virginia, where he was 10-18, and 1950 in Columbia, South Carolina (15-7). While in Columbia, he threw a no-hitter against the Savannah Indians on the fourth of July. Later that season he was promoted to the Double-A Tulsa Oilers, where he went 2-2. In October of 1950 his contract was purchased by the Triple-A Buffalo Bisons in the International League. In his one season in Buffalo he went 11-11 and was sixth in the league with a 2.92 ERA. As was common during that time period, Savransky would miss the next two seasons, 1952 and 1953, while serving in the military. When he returned he was part of a trade that sent him to Cincinnati. He would go on to play in 16 games with the Reds in 1954 where his record was 0-2 with an ERA of 4.88. He went 1 for 2 at the plate with that lone hit coming off of Gene Conley of the Milwaukee Braves. In his other at-bat he drew a base on balls. Interestingly, he scored a run on each plate appearance. Now retired, he lives in Boca Raton, Florida.*

What's your family's background?

MS: My folks came from Russia, the Ukraine. My dad came from Odessa and my mother from Kiev. Had my dad been born in this county, he would have been a good athlete. He was well coordinated, strong. He would have been alright. I was the only athlete. Most of my family were musicians and good scholars. My one brother was an attorney in Cleveland. In fact, he was a partner in the law practice with Dan McCarthy, who took over as interim president of the Yankees when George Steinbrenner had that problem with Major League Baseball.

Tell me a little bit about your early years and how you got involved in baseball.

MS: I was born on January 13, 1929 during the depression in Cleveland, Ohio. I was the youngest of six children, three boys and three girls. There was an oldest boy who passed away when he was young. I grew up in Cleveland, and in my junior high days at Alexander Hamilton Junior High in Cleveland, we moved up to Cleveland Heights. I went to Roosevelt Junior High School, and I played basketball and just about every kind of sport there was. Then I went to Cleveland Heights High School and I played basketball, baseball, and football. I was very thin, didn't weigh much, and I got the heck beat out of me. At one point I got a concussion. I got kicked in the head, and I said, "That's not for me." Not for a nice Jewish boy to be in that game, so I stuck with the basketball and the baseball, and I wound up going to Ohio State. I really went on a basketball scholarship, but I played basketball and baseball over there. That was the first year that all the servicemen came back, 1947, and so we had to play freshman ball. You couldn't play varsity. After my first year there, I signed to play professional baseball, so I couldn't play basketball or anything there. I was no longer an amateur.

Going back to your high school years, you were a very good pitcher there. Weren't you part of a state championship at Cleveland Heights?

MS: In my whole high school career, I lost one game. I lost a game to Shaker Heights High School, which was our arch rival. I went to Cleveland Heights, and my cousin went to Shaker Heights, and I lost that game 3-2. My senior year we won every game and, of course, we won the state championship that year, the only state championship they ever won in baseball. In fact, not too long ago, I was back in Cleveland. They had us in to induct our team and me into the Hall of Fame from Cleveland Heights High. The school's a hundred and two years old now, and it was very nice. All these years went by and they had never done anything like this, so now they did it.

So once you graduated high school, you headed out for college, to Ohio State, to play basketball?

MS: Right. I went down there right out of high school, to Ohio State, in 1947. I would go away in the spring and go to spring training, but I continued my education even though I eventually gave up my amateur standing. Our basketball team, the freshman team, was pretty good. Ohio State won the Big Ten that year, and we used to play them every day in practice, and we used to beat them. We had a heck of a freshman team. I was only 5'11" and weighed 150 pounds, and I could dunk, jump, and I could run fast, but baseball was my real sport that I loved. I liked basketball, but to me baseball was everything. In 1947 after I graduated to high school, I was chosen to represent the Middle West in this game called "Brooklyn against the World" All-Star game. My team was made up of pick-ups from all over the country that they had chosen, and we played against the best of all the burroughs in New York. It was sponsored by the Brooklyn Eagle and the Brooklyn Dodgers, and Branch Rickey was there, of course. I played in there and I had a no-hitter against them for seven innings, up in Ebbets Field, and that's when all the scouts tried to sign me. I was solicited pretty highly, and I wound up signing with Cincinnati. In 1948 I signed a Major League contract, and they gave me a pretty fair bonus, which for that time was a lot of money but nothing compared to what they get today. I got like an eighteen thousand dollar bonus, and in 1948 that was a lot of money.

What did your parents think of your desire to become a professional baseball player?

MS: Well, my dad was in the petroleum business and in real estate and he said to me, "I don't want to stop you if that's what you want, go ahead and do it. I wouldn't want you to always think I begrudged you letting you go into it." When I went into it they didn't object. My dad always said, "If you'll put that same time you put into baseball into my business, you'll make more money in the long run," and he probably was right because we didn't get the kind of money they get today.

Since you had already started at Ohio State, did your parents push you to make sure that you finished your college education?

MS: Yes, they kind of encouraged me.

So once you sign with the Reds, where were you assigned to first?

MS: Well, I went with Cincinnati. I joined the ball club over the fourth of July, and I signed on the twenty-ninth. I met the ball club in Pittsburgh at Forbes Field in 1948, and I roomed with Johnny Vander Meer, which was a great thrill for me. He's the only man that ever threw two consecutive no-hitters in the big leagues. I almost did it in the minor leagues when I was with Columbia, South Carolina in the South Atlantic League, the Sally League, which was a Class-A league. I pitched four consecutive shutouts. The first one was a four-hit shutout, the next one was a two-hit shutout, the next one was a no-hit shutout, and the fourth one was a one-hit shutout. They wanted to bring me up, but Pat Patterson, who was the head scout for the Reds, said, "He's young. Let him get the experience, let him stay down there." I was young, but I was ready, and they didn't bring us up like they do today where you don't need all that experience. But I never regretted it, and I came up in due time. At the end of every season I would go up, and in 1951 I was with Buffalo, New York in the International League, and I had a good year there. I think I went 14-7 or 15-7, and I had a .225 earned run average, and they had some great ball players in Triple-A in those days. Anyway, I came up at the end of the season with Cincinnati and was supposed to go to spring training, but before I could go I was drafted into the Army for the Korean War, and I put in my time there. Then I joined the ball club, and I was with them in 1953 and 1954. I had hurt my arm in the Army and had bone chips cut out, so in 1955 I wound up going to Seattle in the Pacific Coast League. I played there for awhile for Freddie Hutchinson. He was the manager there and later became the manager of the Reds, and he pitched for the Detroit Tigers way back when. From there I finished out that season with Charleston in the American Association.

What was it like to be a young Jewish kid leaving home to go out and play professional baseball in the early 1950's? What about some of those towns you played in?

MS: Well, my first year in baseball I encountered the most anti-Semitism I ever did. There were actually a couple of places where I had problems. One was in Hagerstown, Maryland, that was in that Central League. In fact, the fellow that gave me a little trouble was Hal Keller, the brother of Charlie "King Kong" Keller who played for the Yankees. Hal was a catcher in the Washington organization. He came up with Washington and he gave me a little problem, but I didn't say anything. The next time he came to bat, I leveled him with a fastball, and then I threw him a curveball, and he jumped out of the way for strike two. Then I leveled him again and I think he got the message. I told him, "You're lucky that's all I did was knock you down. If I ever hear any of that crap from you again, you're going to get it good. I won't be so kind as to miss you." After that I never had any trouble with him. When I played in that town in Pennsylvania, I can't think of the name of that town, they were in the league too. They had somebody sitting right behind the dugout giving me a lot of problems, and I told him, "I can't do anything to you in the ballpark. You paid your way in." His wife was with him, and I said to him, "When this game is over, you better get in your car in a hurry because I'm going out after you." And I ran right out there after the game, and he got in his car, locked the doors, put the car in reverse, and almost hit a woman, just brushing her. That was the last time I ever saw him at a ball game. I guess he got enough and that was it, but there were a lot of people that were very bigoted. A lot of people didn't know what a Jew was. They thought we had horns or something. We were like anyone else. We were just trying to do what we had to do and make it.

What do you remember about the first time you got called up to Cincinnati and the first time you played in a Major League game?

MS: I was thrilled, I really was, and I was as nervous as can be. But the first time I got into a ball game, I came into a game in Chicago, in Wrigley Field, and my heart was pounding like a drum. I was so nervous, but I did alright. Then the next time that I pitched, I pitched in a game that was very memorable for me. We were playing the Phillies in Shibe Park. At that time the A's and the Phillies both used Shibe Park and in the first inning our leadoff man for us, Bobby Adams, the second baseman, he led off the ball game with a home run into the left field stands. It was against Robin Roberts, who was a pretty fair pitcher. I came into the game when the score was three to one, they were ahead three to one, and I pitched three perfect innings. I didn't give up anything, and we lost the game three to one, but that was quite an honor for me. They put in a pinch-hitter for me believe it or not; they didn't know I was that good of a hitter then. In any event, we lost the game, but it was memorable for me.

You only had two at-bats in the major leagues. Tell me about those.

MS: I was a pretty good hitter for a pitcher. I hit .300 in Triple-A. I didn't bat that many times in the big leagues. I have a .500 batting average, one for two, but I had a rarity. I scored more runs than I had at-bats because I walked and somebody bunted me over and I scored. The one hit I got in baseball I got off of a big right-handed pitcher that played pro basketball, too, Gene Conley. I could run, and I hit a high bounder to the left side, towards the shortstop, and I legged it out for a hit.

What were your thoughts when you decided to end your career? You did stay connected for a while by assisting the Indians by throwing batting practice, but did you ever have any thoughts of ever trying to make it back?

MS: I had a nice career while it lasted, but it's surely a shame that it had to get cut short. Today, with the medicine and the medical treatment, I would have never had these problems. My arm was good. Actually, I got a lot of these bone chips from throwing the screwball. Of course, you throw the curveball one way and you turn the ball the opposite way to throw the screwball. My manager my first year in baseball was Joe Beggs. He was a relief pitcher for the Yankees back maybe in the 1940's, and he's the one that got me to start throwing the screwball. I don't recommend it. It's tough on the arm. They were just beginning to throw the slider then. I started trying it. Had I stayed in baseball, I probably would have used the slider. So I had the fastball, the curveball, and the changeup and would have had the slider. I had the screwball too. I'd had an operation in 1956, and they cleaned out the chips again and I was having problems. I won a game in spring training but still it didn't mean anything, and I wound up going on the voluntary retired list, and I never went back. I used to pitch batting practice for the Indians just about all the time when they were home, and Mel Harder was the pitching coach, and he said, "Moe, you got good stuff. You should come back and play." But I had got into business with my dad, and I got married, and I figured, "Well, I've had it," but I really could have gone back. My arm came around pretty good. The Indians were pretty good in those days, and I could get them out in batting practice, and I didn't throw hard in batting practice. I had a very good curveball. It dropped right off the end of the table. I threw it just like Warren Spahn, but had I not hurt my arm, I think I would have had a real good career.

As you look back on your time in baseball, who were some of the great players that you had the pleasure to either play with, against, or just get to know?

MS: Well, of course, at Cincinnati we had some really nice ball players. We had Ted Kluszewski, we had Gus Bell, who was Buddy Bell's father. We had Roy McMillan at shortstop, Johnny Temple at second base. They're all gone now. I think Grady Hatton is still living, he was the third baseman. Bobby Adams was the utility infielder. The left fielder was Jim Greengrass; he lives in Atlanta. We got him from the Phillies. He was a nice guy, a tough kid. In center field we had Wally Post, and in right field Gus Bell, and I think they switched around sometimes. Joe Nuxall was the youngest player ever in the big leagues and they changed the law because of that. He was only fifteen years old. I roomed with Joe, and Joe was a real nice guy. I knew his brother too as a pretty fair softball player. I played against some of the best. I played against Stan Musial. I played against Ted Williams in an exhibition game because he was in the American League. I played against the Dodgers when they had some pretty fair ball players. I played in a great era.

You had your picture taken with Cy Young. Where and when did you get to meet him?

MS: In 1948 when I signed with the Reds, and then they sent me out to Sunbury in the Central League, it was the night that Babe Ruth died. I pitched that ball game, and they called time out and had everybody bow their heads in reverence: "We've lost Babe Ruth tonight," and there was a moment of silence. But that night Cy Young was in the dugout and they took a picture of Cy Young with his arm around me. I didn't know what memorabilia it would be; do you think I ever got it signed? I never even got him to sign it. I was never big on memorabilia; I didn't know anything about it. My kids have the picture. I have a picture of Babe Ruth. I wasn't in the picture. It was Babe Ruth and Lou Gehrig, and I never got that signed.

Did you ever meet either Ruth or Gehrig?

MS: I met Babe Ruth one time when he was sick. He came into Cleveland and he had cancer already. He had on that beautiful camel hair coat and wore that tan hat that he used to wear. I remember him very well. He was losing weight, and he was looking bad, but it was a pleasure just to meet him.

From what I've heard, when you gave up baseball you turned your competitive spirit on to playing softball.

MS: After I got done playing pro ball, I played slow-pitch in the major slow-pitch in world tournaments and everything. I was a pretty good hitter, and I played pitcher, catcher, and first base, whatever. I enjoyed all my athletic endeavors. If I had it to do over again, I wouldn't do anything any different. I led a very interesting life. I've done a lot of things, and like I say, it was quite an experience. A lot of my friends sometimes kid me and tell me, "You're a has-been," and I always say, "Better to have been a has-been than a never-was," and that's the way I felt about it.

*"What I wanted to be was the best. I was quoted one time as saying,
'I want to be a Jew that, when he walks down the street,
every other Jew can be proud of him.'
That's kind of the way I felt and I feel that today."*

AL ROSEN

Al Rosen

When listing the all-time greatest Jewish ballplayers, right there along with Hank Greenberg and Sandy Koufax is the name **Albert Rosen**. Rosen played his entire ten-year career with the Cleveland Indians. He earned the nickname "Hebrew Hammer" for his ability to put bat to ball in the major leagues. He was born in Spartanburg, South Carolina on February 29, 1924. Three years later, to better deal with his childhood asthma situation, the family moved to Florida and settled in Miami. Rosen learned the game playing baseball and softball on Miami's sandlots, while at the same time building his toughness as an amateur boxer. Action in the ring resulted in his nose being broken numerous times. In 1941, Rosen attended the University of Florida where he played third base for the Gators. His college career, however, was cut short when he decided to enlist in the Navy following Japan's bombing of Pearl Harbor. He spent two years in the Pacific. He returned from the service and to baseball in 1946 and found a spot with the Pittsfield Electrics, a team in Massachusetts that was a member of the Canadian-American League. In his one season there, he led the league with 16 home runs and 86 RBI's while hitting .332. In 1947 he moved on to Oklahoma where he played for the Oklahoma City Indians in the Texas League. Oklahoma City was a Minor League affiliate of the Cleveland Indians. His bat was just as potent as he hit .349 with 186 hits, 141 RBI's and a slugging percentage of .619. Based on those numbers he was named the MVP of the league and earned a late season call-up to Cleveland, making his Major League debut on September 10, 1947. He was twenty-three years old. In 1948 he was promoted to Triple-A Kansas City in the American Association where he had such a good season he was chosen as the league's Rookie of the Year. Again in 1948 he was a late-season addition to the roster in Cleveland and was fortunate enough to be a part of the Indians World Series championship. With established third baseman Ken Keltner on the roster, Rosen had to wait until 1950 before reaching the majors on a full-time basis. When he did, he showed everyone that he was more than ready to handle big league pitching. In his first full season in Cleveland, he led the American League, hitting 37 home runs with 116 RBI's while batting .287. At that time that was the most home runs ever hit by a rookie. In 1953 Rosen *enjoyed his best season offensively while just missing out on the Triple Crown. He hit .336 and finished second to the Senator's Mickey Vernon, who hit .337. As a consolation, his league-best 43 home runs and 145 RBI's earned him the American League Most Valuable Player Award. He certainly enjoyed the 1954 All-Star game when, despite playing with a broken finger, he hit consecutive home runs and was named the game's MVP. Following a solid season in 1955, Rosen struggled with injuries and retired at the end of the 1956 season. In his ten seasons he had a career batting average of .285 with 192 home runs and 717 RBI's. He was a four-time All-Star, had a World Series ring, and an American League MVP award. After working in the financial field for a number of years, Rosen returned to the game in a front office capacity working with the Yankees (1978-79), the Astros (1980-85) and Giants (1985-92). He is a member of not only the Cleveland Indians Hall of Fame but also the National Jewish Sports Hall of Fame, the International Jewish Sports Hall of Fame as well as the Texas League Hall of Fame. He lives in Rancho Mirage, California.*

Tell me about your early years growing up. You were raised by your mother, grandmother, and your aunt. Was your father not with the family?

AR: I really have no recollection of any place other than South Florida, the southwest section of Miami. That's the earliest that I could really be coherent about anything. It is a typical story. It was during the depths of the Depression, and my father left when my brother and I were very young. I was six and my brother was two and my mother moved in with her mother and sister, and we lived together for a number of years in Miami.

As you were growing up during these years and you become active in sports, when did you begin to feel like baseball was something special for you?

AR: I remember loving to play anything with a ball: baseball, basketball, softball, football. We played them all. In those days you could allow your children to go down to the playground or wherever it might be, the ball field, and feel relatively safe that they'd be coming home. It was different than it is today. That's what kids did in those days. We had nothing else to do. There were no fancy bicycles. We all had one bike per family. There were no thrills in my growing up. I had a working mother and a working aunt. My grandmother took care of the house. My brother and I played anything with a ball constantly whether it was at the playground, in the streets or in the backyard. I continued to play. I played American Legion baseball. I played softball quite a bit. I played in men's leagues from the time I was thirteen and knew that in my heart of hearts that I wanted to be a baseball player. I was able to fulfill that.

As good as you were at playing baseball, it was not your only sport. Tell me about your time competing as an amateur boxer.

AR: Well, you know, I was sort of a gym rat. I used to hang out at the gyms in Miami and watch fighters. I remember a fighter that was very nice to me named Petey Sarron. That's what kids did. There was nothing else. We didn't have the internet, we didn't have Game Boys. We did things that were of interest to us because that's all there was. I did some boxing in the Navy and at the Florida Military Academy, which was noted for its boxing program. I also represented a fraternity at the University of Florida and won the middle weight boxing championship there. Then I went into the service and I used to spar and things like that down in the hole in the ship and we put on some shows in those days. Different ships would dock someplace and they'd have a boxing team on their ship, you'd have one on your ship and that's what that was all about. I loved it, but it was nothing that I ever thought about doing as a career.

At some point you knew you were a better than average player because you wound up at the University of Florida and earned a roster spot with the Gators.

AR: Well, I went to the University of Florida because it was the state school. Because of my softball abilities, I got a scholarship at the Florida Military Academy in St. Petersburg. Playing softball I met a man by the name of J.D. Lemon, whose son went to Florida Military Academy, and they were embarking on an athletic program trying to bring more notoriety to the school and they were giving out scholarships. Mr. Lemon asked me if I would be interested in going to FMAN. I told my folks and, of course, we were ecstatic about it. So that was due to the fact that I was a pretty good softball player and played in a men's league, a traveling league, representing the city of Miami Beach.

Now you were only at the University of Florida for one year. What happened?

AR: I went to Florida one year and then December 7th happened. I knew I was going to go into the service but prior to enlisting, which I did in September of 1941, I wanted to play one year of baseball. I guess I got that terrible itch to play and I was a walk-on at Thomasville, North Carolina in the North Carolina State League. It was $90.00 a month, but I had the experience of playing for a great manager, an excellent hitter who took a real interest in me. He used to throw a lot of batting practice to me in the mornings before games. So, I did get that one year in and I'm eternally grateful for that. After that I went back to my home in Miami and enlisted at the University of Miami where I went into the B-12 program. I stayed in school for a little while and then I went to Officer Training School. I came out as an ensign and was sent down to Fort Pierce, Florida and from there I went overseas.

Even as recent as the late 1960's we saw players having to take time off from their teams for monthly reserve training. It's certainly something that the modern day ballplayers don't even think about. What was that like for you to have to put your career on hold and go off to World War II?

AR: Well, I was like every other kid who loved his country. I knew that it was my duty and responsibility and my desire to do whatever I could to protect this great country and that was the reason for my enlistment. In all probability, had I not enlisted, I would have been drafted so time in the service was a duty that most able-bodied men performed because they wanted to.

Talk to me about your time in the Navy. What kinds of action were you involved in?

AR: I became a small boat officer in charge of the LCVP's (Landing Craft, Vehicle, Personnel) aboard our ship. Our ship was an attack transport, the USS *Procyon* AKA-2 and we made the initial landing at Okinawa. We were there that Easter Sunday the kamikazes came over. We were fortunate. We took the troops and materials into the beach, landed them, went back out and continued to do that. Every night the convoy would go out into the ocean someplace away from shore and away from unfriendly fire. In that regard I was very fortunate. But I did make the one landing at Okinawa and I was in the fleet that was heading towards Japan when the war ended due to the dropping of the atom bombs.

You came out of the service in 1946 and went right back into baseball. You went to Pittsfield, Massachusetts and played with the Pittsfield Electrics.

AR: I was in Pittsfield, Massachusetts in the Canadian-American League. I did not realize at the time, but Thomasville in the North Carolina State League had a working agreement with Cleveland. Therefore, I became Cleveland property and that's how I went to the Cleveland Indian's spring training for their Minor League teams. That was in South Carolina. I was assigned to their Class-T Pittsfield team and I played the season there.

You played well enough in Pittsfield to earn a promotion to Oklahoma City, their Double-A affiliate in the Texas League.

AR: Yes, I played in the good old Texas League. Obviously I enjoyed every minute of it because I was having one of those years. The people I like to think about, at my age I cannot remember very much about it anymore. I do recall that at the end of that season the Cleveland Indians called me up for a "cup of coffee." I spent the last few weeks with the team. I met Bill Veeck, who was the owner of the club at the time. I met some good players. I did strike out my first time at bat and that was my introduction to the big leagues. I must tell you that I made my debut in Yankee Stadium, so you can imagine what was going on in my heart, my stomach and my mind.

Do you remember what it was like as you were walking to the plate for that first at-bat?

AR: Well, it's hard to remember today, but I can guarantee you I was overjoyed and in awe.

In 1948 you moved up to Triple-A Kansas City in the American Association where you had a great season and won Rookie of the Year honors. You were also called up again late in the season to Cleveland and were fortunate enough to be a part of their World Series team.

AR: Again, I was called up. I'd gotten hurt the third week in August and Bill Veeck, who sort of took a liking to me, had the club call me up. They activated me for the World Series. I made one appearance, I popped out. You can imagine what it is like. You're on a club, actually on a twenty-five man roster of the team that won the world championship. I've never forgotten it. I've never forgotten some of the players on that club that are distant memories now for a lot of people, but they were great players in their day. When we got back from winning, we'd played in Boston against the old Braves, I've never been subjected to any kind of happy, riotous and joyous time. The people of Cleveland turned out and we had a parade. It was just typical old time kind of stuff that you rarely see anymore.

In the time you spent with the Indians as a September call-up in 1948, did you get a chance to know Satchel Paige at all? Paige made his Major League debut with the Indians in July of that year.

AR: He was a teammate for a short time, but I did not know him well.

Ken Keltner was the starting third baseman between 1947 and 1949, but you were finally able to take over the position on a full time basis in 1950.

AR: Well, it became obvious to management that maybe Kenny had reached that point and they also had me and they had used up all my options, so it was a matter of me having to stay with the club or they would have had to deal me or release me. I think it was maybe three of four days before spring training was over they released Keltner and inserted me at third base and that is how I began my Major League career.

As I looked at your offensive numbers, you seemed to adjust to Major League pitching rather quickly following your seasons in the minors

AR: Well, you gained experience and you're playing with people who are awfully good players. You don't knock in runs unless you have people like Al Smith, Dale Mitchell, or a Larry Doby or a Bobby Avila hitting in front of you. And then you have to have somebody in back of you. We had pretty good lineups, and I was lucky to have good players hitting in front of me and in back of me. You may get credit for individual numbers but it really is a team effort. In baseball nobody can stand up there all by himself and knock in runs unless they've got people on base.

In 1953 you had the best year of your career and came within one percentage point of baseball's Triple Crown. What was going on with you throughout that season?

AR: There's no doubt 1953 was a great year for me. I had some pretty good years before that, and I'm proud of the fact that it took a long time for Mark McGuire to break my American League rookie home run record. I had 37 home runs in 1950. The unfortunate thing was that in 1954 I was off to an even better start when I got hurt, and from there on my career just took a downturn and I never recovered from it.

What kinds of injuries were taking their toll?

AR: My right index finger, which is still stiff today, was not handled properly. I couldn't swing the bat as well as I could before. I was so prideful of my career that I didn't want to be just another player. The day before spring training, I was taking my young son over to see my brother in Miami and I got rear-ended. You know, I hear people talk about whiplash, but until you have one you really don't know what pain is. So that year was a terrible year for me. I couldn't play the way I was accustomed to playing, and I decided that if I couldn't be what I took great pride in being, then I had to do something else. I could not walk out on the field and be less than I wanted for myself.

Considering the time period that you played, as a Jewish player, I'm guessing that you heard your share of anti-Semitic insults either from other opposing players or from the crowd. From your reputation, it was apparently well known that you were not going to sit by and listen to it without rebuttal.

AR: I was very proud to be a Jew. If anybody cast aspersions on the fact that I was a Jew, if the situation called for it, I did something about it. The thing I found all through the minor leagues is that there are people who cast aspersions on anybody who's different than they are. You know, I saw guys take real verbal beatings because they wore glasses or because they were red-headed and had freckles. I saw guys take verbal beatings over such minor things that today they seem to be so juvenile that it's difficult to talk about. But, there is no doubt that there was anti-Semitism and there were people who shouted out from the stands and there's no doubt that players on other teams did that. I did the best I could, and if I felt there was something that was out of line, I made sure that the person who I felt was out of line had to answer to me. It never occurred to me whether the guy was bigger or smaller. It was a mind game. I just felt that I was proud to be a Jew and I didn't want anybody casting aspersions about the fact that I was Jewish. If they didn't like the way I looked, that was one thing. If they didn't like the way I played, that was one thing. My religion was mine with great pride and I just wouldn't back down.

Being a young Jewish player in 1947, what were your thoughts as you saw Jackie Robinson doing what he was doing in breaking the color barrier?

AR: I thought it was such a huge turnaround in the fabric of America. At the time I was almost speechless. I played with Larry Doby when he was making his way in the American League and I thought the job he did, and I saw that first hand, was just absolutely magnificent. He handled situations and some of them were very difficult. It was a crowning achievement in American sports.

During that era, when there were so few Jewish ballplayers, was it something you took extra pride in, the fact that you were among a select few to reach the Major League level?

AR: What I wanted to be was the best. I was quoted one time as saying, "I want to be a Jew that, when he walks down the street, every other Jew can be proud of him." That's kind of the way I felt and I feel that today. In my life I live today I'm still very proud. Of course, things have changed for Jews and Jewish ballplayers since 1946 and for the State of Israel. That was a real turnaround for people in the public eye. But I've always felt that I wanted people of my faith to be proud of me and I wanted people to generally respect me. They don't have to like me, but respect is different.

You knew Hank Greenberg because he was the General Manager of the Indians while you were there. What was he like as a person?

AR: Yes, he was the General Manager when I went up in 1948. He was with them then and in 1958 or 1959 he left the Indians and later went over to the White Sox.

Hank was a great player, the greatest player of his generation. He was a fine gentleman. He served his country well and I want to leave it right there.

You decided to retire following the 1956 season and from there you went into the financial services industry, getting into the brokerage business. You were in that business for twenty years before you returned to baseball in a front office capacity.

AR: Well, I was never really far from the game. I began in the brokerage business when I was still playing in Cleveland because I wanted to make my home in Cleveland. Rather than going back to Miami and doing the back and forth kind of thing, I always felt there had to be life after baseball. I remained in the brokerage business, had some great people including George Steinbrenner and I stayed in the business with a firm that is no longer in existence called Bache Company in Cleveland.

So what brought about your return to baseball after all that time? You were out of the game for about twenty years at that point.

AR: Gabe Paul was the General Manager of the New York Yankees when George Steinbrenner bought the club in 1973. Gabe had gone over there with him. Then, one of the stockholders with the Yankees, a fellow named F. J. O'Neill, bought the Cleveland Indians, sold his stock in the Yankees, asked Gabe, his good friend, to come back and run it for him and he went back to Cleveland. Then George asked me if I would come back and run the Yankees, become President of the Yankees. I did that. I took over September 1, 1977 and I left in 1979. As everybody knows George and I were always good friends, but I couldn't work for him. That's when I left and I went from there to Houston. I stayed in Houston through the 1984 season. Bob Lurie hired me as the President and General Manager of the Giants and that's where I was until the end of 1992 when I retired.

Who would you say was the toughest pitcher you faced?

AR: Allie Reynolds. He was a big tough guy and he never forgot a base hit that you'd gotten off of him. He would come inside and he could throw. He was the toughest I ever faced.

Who were some of the great players you got to play alongside or maybe even against?

AR: I'll talk about the guys on our club. Lou Boudreau. Joe Gordon was such a tremendous influence on me. I'm so delighted he got into the Hall of Fame. He certainly is deserving. He was deserving for many, many years. I remember, with great fondness, people like Bobby Avila, Ray Boone, Larry Doby, Al Smith, Dale Mitchell, and Bob Kennedy, who followed me and worked for me all through my baseball career. I was lucky. I met some terrific people all along the way. It's a crowning achievement to have played with those people.

Which ballparks did you enjoy playing in the most?

AR: Well, I always wondered what it would be like to hit in Fenway Park all season. Old Municipal Stadium in Cleveland was a good ballpark and the rest of them, you know, you remember them if you had good days there and you don't like them if you don't. I never had any favorites. I must say that, as a right-handed hitter, going into Fenway Park was always something you looked forward to.

As the news and names continue to come out with regards to the players of the so-called "Steroid Era," for a guy who put up impressive numbers, what are your thoughts on the stats that some of these guys put up in recent years? Some have suggested putting an asterisk next to their names and statistics in the record books.

AR: I don't condone cheating and I think the use of steroids is just that. I'm disappointed in some of the names and in some of the people who have been "outed," so to say. Did they have talent? Yes, they had talent. Would they have been as good without steroids? I don't know. Nobody can look back and say that Mark McGuire would not have hit that many home runs had he not been on steroids, but I abhor the idea that people make a mockery of what I consider to be so important to the fabric of this country. Baseball is very important to people in this country and I just feel that it's wrong. What baseball will do about it is their business. Bud Selig has been a great commissioner. He loses a lot of sleep over this whole issue, knowing him and knowing how passionate he is about the game. So, it's a disappointment and we'll get past it somehow.

Larry Yellen
Career record: 0-0
Games: 14
ERA: 6.23
12 K's

Ron Blomberg
Career batting average: .293
52 HR's
224 RBI's

Elliott Maddox
Career batting average: .261
18 HR's
234 RBI's

Jim Gaudet
Career batting average: .071
14 at-bats
1 hit

Richie Scheinblum
Career batting average: .263
13 HR's
127 RBI's

Joe Ginsberg
Career batting average: .241
20 HR's
182 RBI's

Ross Baumgarten
Career record: 22-36
ERA: 4.00
222 K's

Mike Epstein
Career batting average: .244
130 HR's
380 RBI's

Ken Holtzman

Career record: 174-150
3.49 ERA
1,601 K's

Norm Sherry

Career batting average: .215
18 HR's
69 RBI's

Steve Stone

Career record: 107-93
3.97 ERA
1,065 K's

Steve Hertz

Career batting average: .000
4 at-bats
2 runs scored

Don Taussig

Career batting average: .262
4 HR's
30 RBI's

Norm Miller

Career batting average: .238
24 HR's
159 RBI's

Barry Latman

Career record: 59-68
3.91 ERA
829 K's

Morris Savransky

Career record: 0-2
4.88 ERA
7 K's

Al Rosen

Career batting average: .285
192 HR's
717 RBI's

◇   ◇   ◇

Cal Abrams, 1949 to 1956, Dodgers (Brooklyn), Reds, Pirates, Orioles, White Sox

Lloyd Allen, 1969 to 1975, Angels, Rangers, White Sox

Ruben Amaro, Jr., 1991-1998, Angels, Phillies, Indians

Morrie Arnovich, 1936-1941, 1946, Phillies, Reds, New York Giants

Jake Atz, 1902-1909, Senators, White Sox

Brad Ausmus, 1993 – Present, Padres, Tigers, Astros

Jesse Baker (Michael Silverman), 1919, Senators

Brian Bark, 1995, Red Sox

Ross Baumgarten, 1978-1982, White Sox, Pirates

Jose Bautista, 1988-1997, Orioles, Cubs, Giants, Tigers, Cardinals

Robert "Bo" Belinski, 1962-1970, Angels, Phillies, Astros, Pirates, Reds

Joseph Bennett (Rosenblum), 1923, Phillies

Morris "Moe" Berg, 1923-1939, Brooklyn Robins, White Sox, Indians, Senators,
   Red Sox

Nathan Berkenstock, 1871, Philadelphia Athletics

Bob Berman, 1918, Senators

Cy Block, 1942, 1945-1946, Cubs

Ron Blomberg, 1969, 1971-1976, 1978, Yankees, White Sox

Sammy Bohne (Cohen), 1916, 1921-1926, Cardinals, Reds, Brooklyn Robins

Henry Bostick (Lipschitz), 1915, Philadelphia Athletics

Lou Boudreau, 1938-1952, Indians, Red Sox

Ryan Braun, 2007-Present, Brewers

Craig Breslow, 2005-2006, 2008-Present, Padres, Red Sox, Indians, Twins

Lou Brower, 1931, Tigers

Conrad Cardinal, 1963, Houston Colt .45s

Known Jewish Players

Frank Charles, 2000, Astros

Harry Chozen, 1937, Reds

Tony Cogan, 2001, Royals

Alta Cohen, 1931-1933, Brooklyn Robins, Phillies

Andy Cohen, 1926-1929, New York Giants

Hy Cohen, 1955, Cubs

Syd Cohen, 1934, 1936-1937, Senators

Richard Conger, 1940-1943, Tigers, Pirates, Phillies

Philip Cooney (Cohen), 1905, New York Highlanders

Ed Corey (Cohen), 1918, White Sox

Bill Cristall, 1901, Indians

Harry Danning, 1933-1942, New York Giants

Ike Danning, 1928, St. Louis Browns

Bob Davis, 1958, 1960, Kansas City Athletics

Isaac "Ike" Davis, 2010-present, New York Mets

Harry Eisenstat, 1935-1942, Brooklyn Dodgers, Tigers, Indians

Mike Epstein, 1966-1974, Orioles, Senators, A's, Rangers, Angels

Reuben Ewing (Cohen), 1921, Cardinals

Al Federoff, 1951-1952, Tigers

Eddie Feinberg, 1931-1932, Phillies

Harry Feldman, 1941-1946, New York Giants

Scott Feldman, 2005-Present, Rangers

Samuel Fishburn, 1919, Cardinals

Leo Fishel, 1899, New York Giants

Matt Ford, 2003, Brewers

August G. "Happy" Foreman, 1924, 1926, White Sox, Red Sox

Micah Franklin, 1997, Cardinals

Murray Franklin, 1941-1942, Tigers

Samuel Fuld, 2007, Cubs

Milt Galatzer, 1933-36, 1939, Indians, Reds

Jim Gaudet, 1978-1979, Royals

Mark Gilbert, 1985, White Sox

Myron "Joe" Ginsberg, 1948, 1950-1954, 1956-1962, Tigers, Indians, Kansas City Athletics, Orioles, White Sox, Red Sox, Mets

Keith Glauber, 1998, Reds

Jonah Goldman, 1928, 1939-1931, Indians

Isidore "Izzy" Goldstein, 1932, Tigers

Jake Goodman, 1878, 1882, Milwaukee Cream Cities, Pittsburgh Alleghenys

Greg Goossen, 1965-1970, Mets, Seattle Pilots, Brewers, Senators

Sid Gordon, 1941-1943, 1946-1955, New York Giants, Boston Braves, Milwaukee Braves, Pittsburgh Pirates

John Grabow, 2003-Present, Pirates

Herb Gorman, 1952, Cardinals

Shawn Green, 1993-2007, Blue Jays, Dodgers, Diamondbacks, Mets

Adam Greenberg, 2005, Cubs

Hank Greenberg, 1930, 1933-1941,1945-1947, Tigers, Pirates

Eric Helfand, 1993-1995, A's

Steve Hertz, 1964, Houston Colt .45s

Jason Hirsh, 2006-Present, Astros, Rockies

Ken Holtzman, 1965-1979, Cubs, A's, Orioles, Yankees

Joe Horlen, 1961-1972, White Sox, A's

Brian Horwitz, 2008, Giants

Bill Hurst, 1996, Marlins

Skip Jutze, 1972-1977, Cardinals, Astros, Mariners

Harry Kane (Cohen), 1902-1903, 1905-1906, St. Louis Browns, Tigers, Phillies

Gabe Kapler, 1998-2006, 2008-Present, Tigers, Rangers, Red Sox, Brewers, Rays

Herb Karpel, 1946, Yankees

Bob Katz, 1944, Reds

Ian Kinsler, 2006-Present, Rangers

Alan Koch, 1963-1964, Tigers, Senators

Known Jewish Players

Michael Koplove, 2001-Present, Diamondbacks, Indians

Brian Kowitz, 1995, Braves

Sandy Koufax, 1955-1966, Dodgers (Brooklyn & Los Angeles)

Barry Latman, 1957-1967, White Sox, Indians, Angels, Astros

Jim Levey, 1930-1933, St. Louis Browns

Alan Levine, 1996, 1998-2005, White Sox, Rangers, Angels, Royals, Rays, Tigers

Jesse Levis, 1992-1999, Indians, Rays, Brewers

Mike Lieberthal, 1994-2007, Phillies, Dodgers

Lou Limmer, 1951, 1954, Phillies

Andrew Lorraine, 1994-1995, 1997-2000, 2002, Angels, White Sox, A's, Mariners, Cubs, Indians, Brewers

Elliott Maddox, 1970-1980, Tigers, Senators, Rangers, Yankees, Orioles, Mets

Cy Malis, 1934, Phillies

Moxie Manuel (Mark Manuel), 1905, 1908, Senators, White Sox

Duke Markell (Harry Makowsky), 1951, St. Louis Browns

Jason Marquis, 2000-Present, Braves, Cardinals, Cubs

Ed Mayer, 1957-1958, Cubs

Erskine Mayer, 1912-1919, Phillies, Pirates, White Sox

Samuel Mayer, 1915, Senators

Ed Mensor, 1912-1914, Pirates

Mike Milchin, 1996, Twins, Orioles, Dodgers

Norman Miller, 1965-1974, Astros, Braves

Buddy Myer, 1925-1941, Senators, Red Sox

Sam Nahem, 1938, 1941-1942, 1948, Brooklyn Dodgers, Cardinals, Phillies

David Newhan, 1999-2006, 2007-2008, Padres, Phillies, Orioles, Mets, Astros

Jeff Newman, 1976-1984, A's, Red Sox

Barney Pelty, 1903-1912, St. Louis Browns, Senators

Jacob Pike, 1877, Hartford Dark Blues

Lipman Pike, 1871-1878, 1881, 1887, Troy Haymakers, Baltimore Canaries, Hartford Dark Blues, St. Louis Brown Stockings, Cincinnati Reds, Providence Grays, Worcester Ruby Legs, New York Metropolitans

Jake Pitler, 1917-1918, Pirates

Aaron Poreda, 2009-Present, White Sox, Padres

Steve Ratzer, 1980-1981, Expos

Jimmie Reese (Solomon), 1930-1932, Yankees, Cardinals

Al Richter, 1951, 1953, Red Sox

Dave Roberts, 1969-1981, Padres, Astros, Tigers, Cubs, Giants, Pirates, Mariners, Mets

Saul Rogovin, 1949-1953, 1955-1957, Tigers, White Sox, Orioles, Phillies

Al Rosen, 1947-1956, Indians

Goody Rosen, 1937-1939, 1944-1946, Brooklyn Dodgers, New York Giants

Harry Rosenberg, 1930, New York Giants

Lou Rosenberg, 1923, White Sox

Steve Rosenberg, 1988-1991, White Sox, Padres

Max Rosenfeld, 1931-1933, Brooklyn Dodgers

Simon "Sy" Rosenthal, 1925-1926, Red Sox

Wayne Rosenthal, 1991-1992, Rangers

Marv Rotblatt, 1948, 1950-1951, White Sox

Mickey Rutner, 1947, Philadelphia Athletics

Michael Saipe, 1998, Rockies

Roger Samuels, 1988-1989, Giants, Pirates

Ike Samuls, 1895, St. Louis Browns

Sid Schacht, 1950-1951, St. Louis Browns, Boston Braves

Harold Schacker, 1945, Boston Braves

Henry "Heinie" Scheer, 1922-1923, Philadelphia Athletics

Richie Scheinblum, 1965, 1967-1974, Indians, Senators, Royals, Reds, Angels, Cardinals

Michael Schemer, 1945-1946, New York Giants

Scott Schoenweis, 1999-Present, Anaheim Angels, White Sox, Blue Jays, Reds, Mets, Diamondbacks

Art Shamsky, 1965-1972, Reds, Mets, Cubs, A's

Dick Sharon, 1973-1975, Tigers, Padres

Larry Sherry, 1958-1968, Dodgers, Tigers, Astros, Angels

Norm Sherry, 1959-1963, Dodgers, Mets

Harry Shuman, 1942-1944, Pirates, Philadelphia Blue Jays (Phillies)

Al Silvera, 1955-1956, Reds

Fred Sington, 1934-1939, Senators, Brooklyn Dodgers (Converted to Christianity)

Mose Solomon, 1923, New York Giants

Bill Starr, 1935-1936, Senators

Jeff Stember, 1980, Giants

Adam Stern, 2005-2007, Red Sox, Orioles

Steve Stone, 1971-1981, Giants, Cubs, White Sox, Orioles

Bud Swartz, 1947, St. Louis Browns

Don Taussig, 1958, 1961-1962, Giants, Cardinals, Astros

Bob Tufts, 1981-1982, Giants, Royals

Eddie Turchin, 1943, Indians

Steve Wapnick, 1990-1991, Tigers, White Sox

Justin Wayne, 2002-2004, Marlins

Phillip "Lefty" Weinert, 1920-1924, 1927-1928, 1931, Phillies, Cubs, Yankees

Phil Weintraub, 1933-1935, 1937-1938, 1944-1945, Giants, Reds, Phillies

Josh Whitesell, 2008, Diamondbacks

Ed Wineapple, 1929, Senators

Steve Yeager, 1972-1986, Dodgers, Mariners

Larry Yellen, 1963-1964, Houston Colt .45s

Kevin Youkilis, 2004-Present, Red Sox

Guy Zinn, 1911-1912, 1914, 1915, New York Highlanders, Boston Braves, Baltimore Terrapins

Eddie Zosky, 1991-1992, 1995, 1999, Blue Jays, Marlins, Brewers

ACKNOWLEDGMENTS

The author would like to thank the following for their contributions to this project:

Andrew Harmon – Cover design

Scott Rohr – Interior layout

Meg Buscema – Author photo

Rabbi Steven Lebow – Preface

Steve Greenberg – Foreword

Shannon Pollitz – Editing and proofreading

Lara Smith-Sitton – Editing and proofreading

Susan Toohey – Editing and proofreading

Katie Zeazeas – Topps Company, Inc.

Doug Reid – Baseball cards

Mike Hayes – Baseball cards

Martin Abramowitz – Baseball cards

Autumn Baskin – General assistance

Allison Bartelski – General assistance

Carol Cohen – General assistance

MJ Trahan – General Assistance

Baseball card images courtesy of the Topps Company, Inc. Card images of Jim Gaudet and Morris Savransky courtesy of Jewish Major Leaguers, Inc.

Jewish Major Leaguers, Inc., a not-for-profit organization "Documenting American Jews in America's Game."
Visit online at www.jewishmajorleaguers.org

FURTHER READING

Bernard Postal, Jesse Silver and Roy Silver. *Encyclopedia of Jews in Sports* (New York: Bloch Publishing Company, 1965)

Ron Blomberg with Dan Schlossberg. *Designated Hebrew: The Ron Blomberg Story* (Sports Publishing LLC, 2006)

Erwin Lynn. *The Jewish Baseball Hall of Fame* (Shapolsky Books, 1987)

Peter S. Horvitz and Joachim Horvitz. *The Big Book of Jewish Baseball* (S.P.I. Books, 2001)

Rob Trucks. *Cup of Coffee: The Very Short Careers of Eighteen Major League Pitchers* (Smallmouth Press, 2002)